Hands
and
Hearts

Hands and Hearts

*Intergenerational
Activities
throughout
the Church Year*

Lois J. Johansson

MOREHOUSE PUBLISHING

HARRISBURG / PENNSYLVANIA

Morehouse Publishing, P.O. Box 1321, Harrisburg, PA 17105

Morehouse Publishing is an imprint of Church Publishing Incorporated.

Cover photography by Steve Fielding

Cover design by Corey Kent

Library of Congress Cataloging-in-Publication Data

Johansson, Lois J.
    Hands & hearts : intergenerational activities throughout the church year / Lois J. Johansson.
        p.   cm.
    ISBN-13: 978-0-8192-2208-4 (pbk.)
        1. Fellowship—Religious aspects—Christianity.   2. Intergenerational relations—Religious aspects—Christianity.   3. Church work.   4. Church year—Miscellanea.
I. Title: Hands and hearts.   II. Title.
BV4517.5.J64   2006
268—dc22
                                                                                    2006001317

Printed in the United States of America

06 07 08 09   10 9 8 7 6 5 4 3 2 1

CONTENTS

Learning by Living

One generation will commend your works to another;
they will tell of your mighty acts.

PSALM 145:4

Once upon a time there was a young couple who loved baseball. They had season tickets for the best seats they could afford. They planned their calendar around home games. They kept stats and avidly followed news of each major league player.

After a time, the couple was blessed with twin boys. They would prop up their babies in infant seats to watch The Team on TV. As the babies grew into toddlers, they wore little outfits sporting The Team's logo. By preschool they had learned to cheer and clap, and they were beginning to ask questions like "Who's on first?"

About the time the twins were enrolled in T-ball, dissension crept into the parental ranks. Dad wanted to buy his sons tickets for the games. Mom said the boys weren't old enough to understand what was going on and the money spent on tickets would be wasted. Besides, what fun could she have at the game if she had to watch the twins instead of the The Team?

And so it was that the children grew from small into medium and then into large. They sometimes played ball in the yards of their friends. Mom and Dad continued to attend The Team's games, carefully preserving that adult privilege for the special time when the children would be old enough to understand.

On their eighteenth birthday the twins opened the envelope that contained their first Major League tickets; they were now old enough to attend the real thing, and The Team's opening game of the season was that afternoon. They thanked their parents (for they were polite boys) but said they'd made other plans with friends who weren't sports enthusiasts.

"Besides," they offered, "we don't really understand the game."

Learning as a Church Family

Real baseball fans are always eager to raise up the next generation of enthusiasts—they'd never withhold experience or explanation from children who are hungry to learn about the sport. In the same way, the Church shouldn't offer only peer-related learning opportunities for its children, teens, or adults. Just like baseball, faith is still learned best in the larger context of the family—the congregation—when young and old meet together and share their perspectives. Being together as a church family and exploring throughout the seasons of the Church year while listening to younger and older voices is the essence of intergenerational learning.

You may not have used the word, but in your lifetime you've learned a great many things "intergenerationally." The way you cut your sandwich, fold your socks, store your tools, mulch your plants, address your elders—you likely do these things the way you do because they were taught to you and modeled by your parents, grandparents, and other adults when you were a child.

But when we grow up, it's easy to forget what it was like to be young, and when we're young we have no idea what it's like to be older. It's too easy to believe that how we are now is the way everyone is, and the only way to learn otherwise is to confront difference. In the all-important issues of faith, the Church is the preferred place for this to happen, since we gather in the name of the God who made us and knows us and loves us, each one. By sharing with one another in a community of faith, we learn new ideas and ask new questions. We tap into a new creativity and explore new spiritual paths.

As you travel together through the seasons of the Church year, you'll come to know Jesus more deeply, weaving the rich stories of Scripture into your everyday conversations and ordinary interactions. Wending your way through the gospel in shared activities with people of all ages, you'll find yourself making a journey through the Church year in a new and meaningful way.

The activities in this book are designed for small groups of 3 to 5 people—a group formed by parents and their children, for instance, may also include a grandparent or a family friend. Couples, singles, and teens can form coalitions by joining at least one other person outside their age group. Children under 5 should be cared for separately so that older kids through older adults can focus on their tasks without distraction. Be sure to let the little ones know that when they head to kindergarten, they can take part in intergenerational activities with the rest of their church family too.

Learning Together in Faith

Perhaps the concept of intergenerational learning is new to your congregation; perhaps its practice has diminished over time. If so, there may be some hesitation about offering events based on this interactive learning model. So it's a good idea to make sure that those who come will find it so worthwhile that they'll not only return at each opportunity but enthusiastically bring others. Five sequential steps form the foundation of this learning model. Do your best to follow them as you plan and prepare intergenerational learning events that will elicit positive responses in your church. These steps are key to making each gathering a success as you develop a faith-sharing community. Shortcuts and detours that bypass these steps may lengthen this journey—or cut it short. And the most important time to observe these steps is the first time you offer an intergenerational event.

Step 1: Choose a Bible-centered theme. The designation "intergenerational learning" carries with it the implication of interaction between all ages. In the case of these activities, a Bible base is mandatory. Faith formation goes beyond mere knowledge to belief, with the Word of God as the focal point. So begin by choosing a Scripture passage or precept to explore, which will become the foundation for all other decisions about the activity. Plan each event around an obvious biblical core, using components that support it. Note the Bible passages central to each of the activities in this book.

Step 2: Design tasks that support and develop the theme. We learn not only by seeing and hearing but by doing—and even by speaking. Conversations are a primary goal of these occasions. They may start with very concrete remarks: "How would you cut out this piece?" Or "Do you think we should use blue or purple?" But before you know it, conversations may grow deeper and more meaningful, and you may find yourself exploring real questions of faith as you ask, "I wonder what that phrase means," or exclaim, "I never thought of it that way!" Even newcomers will find it easy to visit while working on a joint project, and soon they're no longer strangers. The task promotes conversation about itself—and about its subject.

Step 3: Find ways for all ages to contribute to the task. No two people are ever equally skilled at the same activities. That disparity is magnified when you ask a group containing three generations to accomplish a task. So it's critical to find a portion of the job that each person is able to do. Try to avoid allowing one or two people in a group to do all the work while others sit idly by. The project itself must involve tasks that are possible for individuals of different developmental levels. Not everyone may be working at the same time—but before the job is finished, each one will have contributed to the finished product. The work-and-rest rhythm lends momentum to each project as members alternately complete the task for which they are most fitted. Interest remains because each has made an investment in what is happening.

Step 4: Encourage lifelong learning. The best activities, like the best sermons, stimulate continuing thought. Encourage participants to view the activity—and the concept—from many sides and to be open to questions that may not have quick or easy answers. Sometimes the activity results in a product—a banner, for instance—that reminds participants of the ideas they've explored and encourages them to keep on pondering. A sense of curiosity and an openness to the creative process—important in all learning—is critical to faith formation.

Step 5: Prepare materials and the environment with care. The road to good participation is paved with good preparation. By attending to detail *before* the event begins, you can maximize participants' time and the church's resources. Visit the area where your activity will take place to be sure it will be suitable. Are the furnishings arranged properly? Is there enough space? Is lighting adequate? And don't forget to check each instruction to make sure it is clear; collect and organize supplies for each area; and test glue bottles and markers, sharpen pencils, and so on. Before the day of the activity, do a trial run with a partner, checking to be sure that no detail has been overlooked.

Using This Book

The activities in this book will help you and your church family implement an intergenerational way of learning. Each event brings together all ages, at home or at church, for spiritual learning among children, youth, adults, and seniors that will be natural, comfortable, and satisfying. All of the activities are designed for a particular place in the liturgical calendar. Each chapter begins with a brief introduction to the Church season for which the activity is designed. Here are some tips to help you get started:

- Adapt these activities to your own church's size and resources.

- Reproducible pages may be photocopied, written on chalkboard or white-board, printed on posters or computer banners, or copied to transparencies for use with an overhead projector.

- Test your materials, and make substitutions if necessary.

- Anticipate traffic. For example, 100 people can be accommodated in the banner-making activity. If you expect more, double up on packets. Prepare another area, scheduling the groups concurrently. Or offer a choice of dates so all can attend. Or distribute packets and invite families to complete their portion of the banner at home.

- Scale back. If your budget and congregation are small, choose to do a portion of an event. For example, you might choose to select fewer banner squares or to make them out of posterboard or construction paper rather than fabric.

- Add resources. If your church has the space, budget, and people to add activities, do so. Stay within the guidelines outlined here.

- Choose one or more activities to offer during this Church year. Each one in this book is independent of the others. You may want to consider a 5-year plan to try each of the activities.

- Children under age 5, whose attention spans and motor skills still aren't fully developed, usually aren't able to successfully engage in these activities. Be sure to set up—and staff—a child-care area so that parents and friends can focus on the tasks at hand.

After completing a few of these events with your congregation, you'll gain an understanding of how to develop or adapt materials for intergenerational learning. Refer to this introduction for guidance and use the above steps as guidelines.

Before you know it, strangers—with their hearts and hands engaged in an enjoyable project—will find themselves turning into friends.

God bless your efforts!

CHAPTER 1

The Waiting Tree

ADVENT

*A shoot will come up from the stump of Jesse;
from his roots a Branch will bear fruit.*

ISAIAH 11:1

The Church year begins with the season of Advent. With joyful expectation, we prepare our hearts for the coming of the Christ child, recalling his birth 2,000 years ago and looking for his return at the end of time. In our Sunday Scripture readings, we listen to the story of Mary's "yes" and to John the Baptist's cry in the wilderness, calling the faithful then—and now—to prepare the way of the Lord with prayer and conversion of heart.

At this event the church family will design, make, and hang miniature life-story books for a Waiting Tree (sometimes called a "Jesse Tree"). The book ornaments will represent Bible characters who waited for a savior. Discussion materials, instructions, patterns, and raw materials will be provided to make decorating this indoor tree possible for ages 5 to 95 in a 1¹/₂-hour session.

The Waiting Tree

Preparation

With a small committee of your choosing, arrange for the following during the month preceding the event.

• Announce the event in the October newsletter and service bulletins.

• Design and delegate room setup.

• Collect and/or buy items for the supplies table.

• Arrange for a pianist to bring hymnals and accompany the hymn.

• Make copies of the worksheet on page 5.

• Make an ornament sample.

• Copy, cut, and fold the character clues (see page 6); place in a basket.

• Arrange for the delivery, potting, and placement of a bare-branched tree.

• Cut tagboard and paper; sharpen pencils; test markers; fill staplers.

• Optional: Arrange care for children under 5; arrange for refreshments.

You Will Need . . .

• One per participant: worksheet, Bible, scrap paper, pencil, scissors (provide child and adult sizes)

• One per group: bottle of craft glue

• Tools: markers, rulers, staplers, single-hole punches, cool-melt glue guns

• Basic booklet: tagboard (22" x 28") cut into 16 pieces (5½" x 7"), assorted colors; white copy paper (8½" x 11"), halved (8½" x 5½")

• Raw materials: scraps (felt, art foam, glossy cardboard, specialty paper); stickers (stars, circles, hearts, animals, flowers, letters); brights (sequins, flat-back "jewels," wiggle eyes, buttons); fancies (feathers, doilies, foil); pictures (church supply catalogs, church-school papers); ribbon (no wider than ¼" and at least 16" long), yarn, multistrand embroidery floss; any extras you wish to add to the project

• Basket of character clue slips

• Bell

Supplies Table

To prevent chaos and facilitate cleanup, put similar items in open boxes, bowls, muffin tins, and so on—fit the container to the category. Many of the raw materials will be left over, but the key is to provide a wide variety.

The Waiting Tree

Welcome [*Hand out worksheets as people enter.*]

Hymn: "Come Thou Long-Expected Jesus"

Introducing the Activity

We've gathered tonight to trim an unusual tree. We call it the Waiting Tree, because the ornaments we'll make for it will remind us of people throughout the Bible who waited for a savior. We'll look at 3 different clusters of these people. First, as the prophet Isaiah mentioned, some of them are from Jesus' family tree. In Isaiah 11:1 the prophet says, "A shoot will come up from the stump of Jesse; from his roots a Branch will bear fruit." You can also track Jesus' ancestors in the genealogies included in Matthew and Luke, which name Joshua, Boaz, and David in his lineage.

Although many of the decorations we'll make tonight will represent these family members, we'll also make symbols for a second group of people who, though not branches of that family tree, were members of the family of faith that waited for the Savior. Many of these men and women are named in Hebrews 11. Among them are Moses, Gideon, and Samson.

The third group of people whose symbols we'll add to the Waiting Tree are those who shared the event of Christ's birth, including John the Baptist, Mary, and the shepherds.

You'll work in groups of 3 or 4 to create an ornament for the character whose name you are about to draw. You're going to make a miniature "life-story book" [*show sample*] for this person. Choose the best symbol for the character and put it on your book cover. Use as many inside pages as you wish for the story. You'll be able to visit the supplies table to gather everything you need.

Just before we have our character drawing, let's review the worksheet you should all have. [*Review instructions, answer questions, and proceed with drawing.*]

We'll ring a bell at intervals to help us track our progress and keep things moving along on time. At the first bell, begin your planning. [*Ring bell.*]

[*Ring bell after 10 minutes.*] Begin to construct your ornament if you haven't already done so. You'll have about 30 minutes. I'll ring a bell after 25 minutes to help you.

[*Ring bell after 25 minutes.*] As you finish, please return tools and leftover items to the table, placing each in its original container. Your assistance will be a great help to our cleanup committee.

[*Ring bell after 5 minutes.*] Now we're ready to trim the tree. Appoint a teller—someone to explain your story—and a trimmer from your group. We'll begin at this table [point]. Please stand by the tree, hold your ornament high, and give us a short (1- to 2-sentence) description of the Bible character it represents.

[*Ring final bell.*] Our Waiting Tree will remain here through the Advent season, after which you may take your ornament. Meanwhile, gladly explain the ornaments to friends and visitors who ask about the tree.

Benediction

Gracious Father, we are in awe of these men and women who waited for salvation. Thank you for the redeeming gift of your Son, Jesus. As we wait for his return, keep us faithful members of your family.

How to Make Your Ornament

- Form a work group of 3 or 4 people, represented by at least 2 different generations. Choose a place to work. Each person should collect a Bible, scrap paper, a pencil, and scissors.

- After you draw your character's name (1 name per group), find and read the Bible references to each other. Discuss other stories or ideas that come to mind when you hear this character's name. Take notes on your scrap paper to help in the next step.

- Plan the design of your ornament, which will be in the form of a "life-story book." You will need to illustrate the cover and inside pages. At the supplies table you will find markers, staplers, tagboard, white paper, miscellaneous scraps, stickers, ribbon, and other items.

- Following patterns on page 7, cut out tagboard cover, white paper pages, and ribbon hanger.

- Fold tagboard so narrow edges meet; crease sharply. Choose items at the supplies table and begin to illustrate the cover. Make sure ornament fold is at left edge.

- Fold pages in half. Illustrate pages using stickers or your own drawings. Stack pages inside cover, matching folds. Staple once at folded edge.

- Insert ribbon into middle of book. Loop so one half is inside and one half is outside on spine of book. Bring ends together above book. Tie ribbon at top book edge and again at ends to form hanger.

- Sign your names and print the date on the back cover. Return unused items to the supplies table.

Abraham—Matthew 1:1–2, 17; Hebrews 11:8; Genesis 17:1–7; 22:17–18

Isaac—Matthew 1:1; Hebrews 11:9, 17, 20; Genesis 22:3–13

Jacob—Matthew 1:1; Hebrews 11:9, 20, 21; Genesis 49:1, 28–33

Jesse—Matthew 1:5, 6, 17; Isaiah 11:1; Acts 13:22–23

David—Matthew 1:1, 5, 6, 17; Hebrews 11:32; 2 Samuel 5:4

Solomon—Matthew 1:6, 7; 1 Kings 3:5–14; 4:29–34; 5:3–5

Joseph—Matthew 1:16, 18–24; Luke 2:1–5

Enoch—Hebrews 11:5–7; Genesis 5:18–24; Jude 14–15

Noah—Hebrews 11:7; Genesis 6:9–22; 9:12–13

Joseph—Hebrews 11:21, 22; Genesis 37:3–50:26

Moses—Hebrews 11:23–28; Exodus 2:1–3:15

Rahab—Hebrews 11:31; Matthew 1:5; Joshua 2:21

Boaz—Matthew 1:5, 6; Ruth 2–4

Joshua—Hebrews 11:29–30, 34; Joshua 1:1–3; 4:1–9; 6:2–20

Gideon—Hebrews 11:32; Judges 6:11–12; 7:1–8, 16–21

Deborah and Barak—Hebrews 11:32; Judges 4:4–10, 14–15; 5:1–3

Samson—Hebrews 11:32, 34; Judges 13:24; 14:5–6; 16:4–5, 18–22, 30

Samuel—Hebrews 11:32; 1 Samuel 3:1–12

Daniel—Hebrews 11:32; Daniel 6:6–23

Angels—Matthew 1:20–21; Luke 1:11–20, 26–38; 2:8–14

Zechariah and Elizabeth—Luke 1:5–79

John the Baptist—Luke 1:62–66, 80; 3:1–4, 11

Mary—Matthew 1:18–21; Luke 1:26–38; 2:4–7

Shepherds—Luke 2:8–20

cover

inside pages

cut ribbon twice this length

CHAPTER 2

A Christmas Carol-Van
CHRISTMASTIDE

Sing to the LORD a new song, for he has done marvelous things; his right hand and his holy arm have worked salvation for him. The LORD has made his salvation known and revealed his righteousness to the nations.

PSALM 98:1–2

The Church moves into the season of Christmastide with joy and celebration as we recall the birth of the Christ child, Emmanuel—God with us. With all Christians, we turn to the Gospel of Luke to read the well-loved story of Jesus' birth. With the angels, we announce his coming—in our world and in our hearts—with songs of wonder and praise.

All ages can make the music of this holy season together. In this activity, we'll imagine that we're a musical caravan as we meet at church and travel to various areas within the building. At each site we'll craft, listen, dramatize, perform, research, or sing the carols of Christmas.

Carol-Van Map

Our musical caravan will travel between the destinations described below.

7:00–7:20

Fellowship Hall   The Journey Begins   Groups will construct "SINGO" game boards for use later on in the evening.

7:20–8:20

Your group may visit the following sites in any order. Each site will accommodate several groups at a time. The destination leader at each site will monitor traffic. You may not have time to attend all 4, so go to your favorites first.

Classroom 1   Good King Drama   Each group will have 2 chances to sing and act out this carol.

Nursery   Cradle Carols Rock   Groups will practice the old German custom of cradling small children while singing "rocking" carols.

Classroom 2   Pray, Play a Lay   Group members will be able to play carols on a musical instrument of their choice.

Classroom 3   Seven Joys Search   Groups will discover the Scripture stories in this ancient carol and learn its refrain.

8:20

Fellowship Hall   The Journey Ends   Groups will reassemble and play SINGO.

The Journey Begins

As participants enter the church, they begin their Carol-Van journey together in this place. Each group of family and/or friends will construct a game board for a musical game of SINGO.

Supplies

Poster board, markers, yardsticks, Christmas card fronts, scissors, glue

Preparation

- Sort card fronts into piles by theme: shepherds, angels, Bethlehem, manger scene, wise men.

- Create a Carol-Van Map displaying all destinations (see sample on page 11).

- Make copies of Worksheet A.

Work Area

Because all participants work together at the same time, this activity requires the largest work area. The fellowship hall or a similar large meeting room is ideal. You'll need a supplies table and other tables at which groups will do their work. A piano will also be needed here at journey's end.

Leader Responsibilities

- Recruit 4 destination leaders and provide them with direction and assistance in advance of the activity.

- Make sure your room is ready.

- Welcome people as they arrive.

- Encourage group formations. A family may be large enough, but singles and couples will need to join a group. Groups work best when they include 4 to 6 people representing at least 2 generations.

- Hand out worksheets and get groups started on task by reading the steps with them.

- Monitor the groups to determine when their game boards are completed. Announce that the remaining itinerary (refer to the Carol-Van Map for destinations) may be completed in any order but that groups are required to stay together. Set a time for the journey to end.

- Monitor traffic between destinations.

The Journey Begins

Welcome to the Christmas Carol-Van. As we imagine ourselves to be a musical caravan, we will wend our way to various destinations in the church, all the while celebrating the birth of Christ our Savior with ancient and modern carols. We will begin our activities in this room and work together. Then we will divide into smaller groups and move to the other destinations at leisure, reassembling here to conclude. Please begin.

1. Form into mixed age groups of 2 to 5 people and find a work space. Everyone in each group should participate in this activity, dividing the responsibilities.

2. Draw a game-board grid for a musical game of SINGO. Take a sheet of poster board, a yardstick, and a marker from the supplies table. Use the yardstick and marker to draw lines dividing the poster board into 16 sections. (Hint: Draw the first line from top to bottom in the middle. Draw the second line from side to side in the middle. Do the same for the 4 new spaces you have created.)

3. Prepare the grid pictures. At the supplies table, pick out one or more Christmas card fronts from each of the sorted piles until you have a total of 16. Take scissors, glue, and card fronts to your work space. Trim the card fronts so each will fit one grid space.

4. Arrange and glue the pictures inside the grid spaces. Talk about the themes the pictures represent.

5. Return the tools and your finished game board to the supplies table; clean your work space and discard all trash.

Now you are ready to travel to a new destination. Refer to the Carol-Van Map to plan your route. You will return to this area at a signal from your leader.

Good King Drama

At this station groups will sing and act out the Wenceslas carol. This activity will be repeated with new groups.

Supplies

Bundle of sticks, crown, tray with dish and glass

Preparation

Make copies of Worksheet B.

Work Area

This activity requires a piano. No chairs are needed, but there should be enough open space so that groups can divide into 3 chorus sections facing a central area where performers can mime the carol.

Leader Responsibilities

• Create 3 groups from those who come, and position them so they can watch the drama unfold.

• Hand out worksheets.

• Choose mimes and hand out props.

• Accompany carol singing.

• Dismiss participants to a new destination; welcome those who come next.

Good King Drama

We will sing and then act out the text of "Good King Wenceslas," written in 1853 by Dr. John Mason Neale.

1. Divide into 3 groups of equal size. Sit or stand facing each other, leaving room in the middle for the action.

2. Group 1 will sing the part of the Narrator, Group 2 the part of the King, and Group 3 the part of the Page.

3. The destination leader will choose a person from each group to pantomime the parts of the poor man, king, and page and will provide props.

4. We'll sing the carol twice. Mimes perform during the second time through.

Note: Pantomime actions appear in bold.

NARRATOR:
   Good King Wenceslas **looked out** on the feast of Stephen,
   When the snow lay round about, deep and crisp and even:
   Brightly shone the moon that night, though the frost was cruel,
   When a poor man **came in sight, gathering** winter fuel.
WENCESLAS:
   "Hither, page, and **stand by me**, if you know it, telling,
   Yonder peasant, who is he? Where and what his dwelling?"
PAGE:
   "Sire, he lives a good league **hence**, underneath the mountain,
   Right against the forest fence, by Saint Agnes' fountain."
WENCESLAS:
   "Bring me food and bring me wine, bring me pine logs hither;
   You and I will see him dine, when we bear them thither."
NARRATOR:
   Page and monarch, **forth they went**, forth they went together;
   Through the rude wind's wild lament and the bitter weather.
PAGE:
   "Sire, the night is darker now, and the wind blows stronger;
   Fails my heart, I know not how: I can go no longer."
WENCESLAS:
   "**Mark my footsteps**, my good page, **tread now in them** boldly;
   You shall find the winter's rage freeze your blood less coldly."
NARRATOR:
   In his master's steps **he trod**, where the snow lay dinted;
   Heat was in the very sod which the saint had printed.
ALL GROUPS:
   Therefore, Christian men, be sure, wealth or rank possessing,
   You who now will bless the poor shall yourselves find blessing.

Now you are ready to travel to a new destination. Refer to the Carol-Van Map to plan your route.

Cradle Carols Rock

Participants will listen to and sing lullaby carols, moving from darkness to light. This activity will be repeated with new groups.

Supplies

CDs of 3 "rocking" (lullaby) carols,*

CD player, working flashlights

Preparation

Make copies of Worksheet C.

Work Area

One or more rocking chairs and/or cradles are needed—consider the church nursery as a resource. Piano or guitar accompaniment for "Silent Night" is optional.

Leader Responsibilities

• Choose (perhaps from oldest and youngest present) who shall rock and who shall be rocked.

• Hand out worksheets and discuss what will happen.

• Turn out room lights; distribute flashlights to shine at appropriate times.

• Operate CD player; shine your flashlight on ceiling at all times.

• Accompany singing of "Silent Night."

• Dismiss participants to a new destination; welcome those who come next.

---

* Such as "Away in a Manger," "Lullay Thou Little Tiny Child," "Rocking Song" (Czech), "Song of the Crib" ("Joseph, dearest Joseph mine . . ."), etc.

Cradle Carols Rock

In the fourteenth-century German tradition of *Kindelwiegen* (when priests and later the people rocked the cradle and sang lullabies to the baby Jesus), we will gather around the cradle or rocking chair and sing Christmas lullabies to the youngest among us.

1. Choose who will rock and who will be rocked. Take your places.

2. The destination leader will play the first rocking carol. You will listen in near darkness.

3. For the second rocking carol, the men will turn on their flashlights. Shine them on the ceiling as you listen.

4. For the third rocking carol, the women will join the men and shine their flashlights on the ceiling. Continue to listen.

5. Finally, the children will turn on their flashlights. When all these lights shine on the ceiling, you will sing together about the night of Christ's birth—silent, calm, and bright ("Silent Night, Holy Night").

6. When the carol is finished, turn off your flashlights, return them to their place, and leave for your next destination in silence.

Please refer to the Carol-Van Map as you make travel plans.

Pray, Play a Lay

At this site everyone will learn to play at least one carol tune on an instrument. This activity will be repeated as new groups come.

Supplies

Melody instruments (church instruments, toys, novelty, single-use),* music stands, elementary band books

Preparation

• Copy piano template on page 20; cut and glue (or tape) as directed.

• Tune bottle band by filling glass bottles so each forms a different note of the scale when lightly struck. Each bottle should have a striker beside it (small ruler, closed pen, etc.).

• Make copies of Worksheet D.

Work Area

Chairs and tables for the instruments and at least one piano (with bench) are needed.

Leader Responsibilities

• Organize the room with plenty of space around each instrument; set up music stands and chairs; prepare music.

• Position keyboard template on the piano, with "1" at middle C.

• Hand out worksheets.

• Dismiss participants to a new destination; welcome those who come next.

---

* Church instruments: piano, chime bells, tone bells, autoharp. Toys: step-on keyboard, tuned blocks or bells, xylophone. Novelty: bottle band. Single-use: kazoos, nose flutes.

Pray, Play a Lay[*]

Music reader or not, you are invited to play at least one carol tune on either a common or an unusual instrument.

Directions

1. Explore the room to learn what instruments are available.

2. If you do not read music, you may still choose to play the piano. With the help of our handy numbered guide, you can teach yourself to play a carol tune.

3. Music readers may play one of the other instruments. Carol melodies are located on music stands near the instruments.

4. Play-it-by-ear musicians may try any instrument and play any carol.

5. You may play as many instruments as time and availability allow.

Your destination leader will monitor the time. Refer to the Carol-Van Map to plan your route.

---

[*] *Lay* is a word with probable Celtic origins meaning a song, especially the tune.

PIANO TEMPLATE   *Destination Leader: Copy this page. Trim off these instructions. Glue remaining page to cardboard. Carefully cut out and remove shaded area. Prop on piano, with first notch fitting over middle C and last notch at higher C.*

1. With one finger of your right hand, evenly play the keys below the numbers in this order:

8 7 6 5 4 3 2 1

2. Now evenly play the keys below the numbers in this order:

8 8 7 6 5 5 4 3 3 2 2 1 1 1

3. Play them again, but do not strike numbers inside parentheses—just "think" them while you hold the key down.

8 (8) 7 6 5 (5) 4 3 (3) 2 (2) 1 (1) (1)

Name that tune!

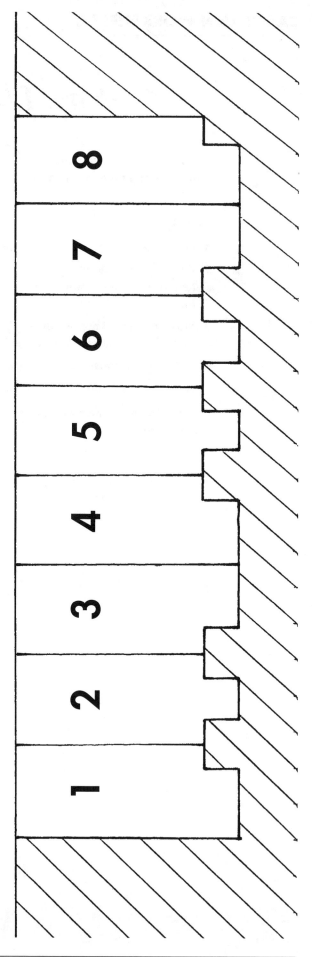

Seven Joys Search

Participants will research and uncover the biblical roots of the stanzas of the Old English carol "The Seven Joys of Mary." After each stanza is sung, its Scripture reference will be read and all will sing the refrain. This activity will be repeated when new groups come.

Supplies

Bibles, basket of numbered slips

Preparation

• Write single numbers 1 to 7 on paper slips.

• Rehearse solo stanzas with accompanist.

• Make copies of Worksheet E.

Work Area

This activity requires a piano and chairs.

Leader Responsibilities

• Set up the room with chairs in a semicircle facing the piano.

• Hand out worksheets and Bibles.

• Help participants locate Bible references.

• Teach the refrain to each group.

• Sing each stanza in turn and lead all in the refrain, calling on a reader for the scriptural explanation.

• Dismiss participants to a new destination; welcome those who come next.

Seven Joys Search

Uncover the biblical roots of each stanza of the Old English carol "The Seven Joys of Mary."

1. Take a Bible from the pile and a number from the basket.

2. Match your number with the numbered clue from the clue list below. Find the reference(s) and be prepared to read it to the group.

3. Your leader will sing stanza 1, all will respond by singing the refrain, and the person with clue 1 will read the reference to the group. Continue through the last stanza and refrain.

Traditional   Old English

Clue List

(1) Luke 2:1–7; (2) Matthew 21:14–16; Luke 7:20–23; (3) Mark 10:46–52; (4) Luke 4:14–21; (5) Luke 8:40–42; Luke 9:49–55; (6) John 19:17–18; John 19:25–30; (7) Acts 1:1–11

Now you are ready to travel to a new destination. Refer to the Carol-Van Map to plan your route.

The Journey Ends

All travelers will return to the place where their journey began. They will use the game boards they made earlier to play SINGO, listening for and identifying familiar Christmas carols.

Supplies

Game boards, red construction paper

Preparation

• Cut red construction paper into quarters, providing 8 to 10 playing pieces for each group's game board.

• Make copies of Worksheet F.

Work Area

Use the tables from the first activity. You will need a piano for playing the carol fragments and accompanying singing.

Leader Responsibilities

• Signal when it is time to reassemble the entire group.

• Hand out worksheets and review the game rules printed on them.

• Hand out paper playing pieces.

• Play carol fragments* and accompany subsequent carol singing.

• Pronounce benediction.

---

* Examples: "While Shepherds Watched," "Angels from the Realms of Glory," "What Child Is This?" "As with Gladness Men of Old," "Once in Royal David's City," and others familiar to you. Also feel free to play carols that can fit several categories, such as "Joy to the World" and "O Come, All Ye Faithful."

The Journey Ends

Join with all of us in using our newly made game boards to play SINGO.

Game Rules

Each team of 2 to 5 players needs 1 playing board, 8 to 10 red playing pieces, and playing space (at a table or on the floor).

The game is similar to bingo; the object is to cover a row of game-board spaces (down, across, diagonally) with playing pieces. A space may be covered when a player determines that the carol being played and the picture in a space "match"—for example, when you hear "Angels from the Realms of Glory," cover the picture of an angel (or angels). A playing piece may not be repositioned during a game. Although you may have multiple angel pictures, only cover a second if another angel carol is played during that game.

When a row of 4 pictures has been covered, the team calls out, "Singo!" The winning team chooses a carol for all participants to sing.

After removing the playing pieces, exchange your game board with another group and play again. (Note: The musician may repeat carols from game to game.)

Thank you for joining our Christmas Carol-Van. This concludes our time together here. We encourage you to "carol-van" in your neighborhood or elsewhere as a response to this rehearsal!

CHAPTER 3

Magi-cal Moments

EPIPHANY

Magi from the east came to Jerusalem and asked,
"Where is the one who has been born king of the Jews?
We saw his star in the east and have come to worship him."

MATTHEW 2:1–2

What an amazing journey! The Magi—learned men from the east—travel the long and difficult road to Bethlehem, following a star to the dwelling place of a poor little family. There they find and worship God as a tiny baby. With the entire Church, we move into the season of Epiphany—Christ made manifest to the entire world. As the Magi opened their hearts to see the divine in the Christ child, so, during this special season, do we. Reading the gospel stories of the season, we learn to make our own journeys and discover Christ in our own everyday epiphanies.

We begin this church-wide activity watching and hearing the story of the wise men who followed the star. After considering their gifts and their possible uses, we will turn our thoughts to those in the community whom we may bless with gifts we have gathered to give.

This suggested room arrangement shows the position and movement of the dramatists. Adapt this arrangement to the area where you'll meet. If you feel that you need more space, consider duplicating rooms and personnel to accommodate all who attend.

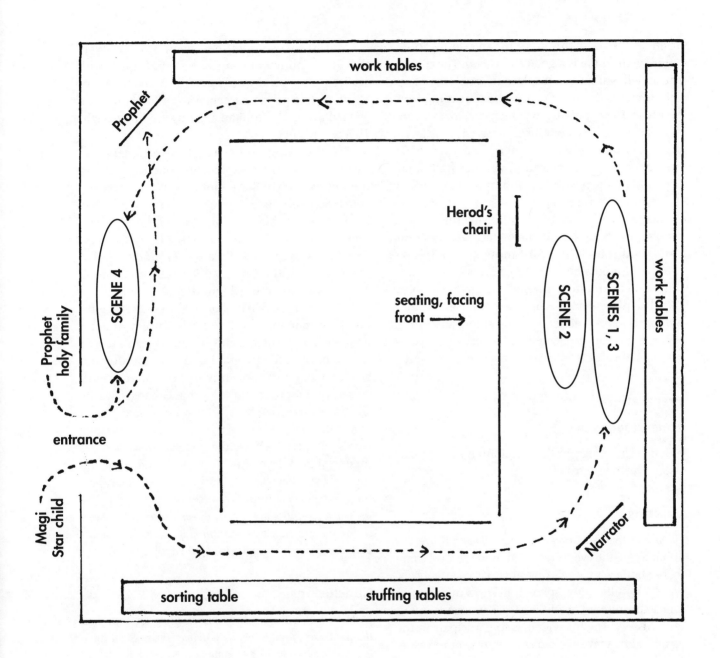

Magi-cal Moments

You may schedule this event for an evening, but a Saturday morning is a good choice too. The congregation will gather in one place to watch the Magical Moments drama, a pantomimed reading from Matthew. Those gathered will then consider why the Magi presented the poor infant Jesus with the lavish gifts of gold, incense, and myrrh. As a response, members of the congregation will decorate small bags and fill them with gifts appropriate for a needy group in the community.

Recruit volunteers for the following roles: narrator, prophet, King Herod, three Magi, Mary, Joseph, child, and star-child. (Ask family groups to take these roles if possible.) Give each actor a copy of the script and the room arrangement diagram (see page 27). The players do not need to rehearse, but they will need to provide their own costume and props. You may prepare and conduct the gift activity yourself or choose an art director to oversee the project.

Preparation

• Arrange the room.

• Gather dramatists in the preparation room; make sure everyone is ready.

Greeting

[*Before dramatists enter, say the following:*] We are about to see the events recorded in the second chapter of Matthew's gospel come alive. Listen attentively, watch carefully, and respond quickly as our narrator and actors remind us of the Magi's moments in our faith history. The first Gentiles to participate in the gospel story, they invested time, effort, and treasure to follow the star, and their devotion brought them to the Savior. [*Introduce narrator; perform scenes 1–4 of the Magi-cal Moments drama.*]

Reflection

[*After dramatists have exited, say the following:*] Gold. Incense. Myrrh. Would you have put those items on your baby's gift registry?

And how wise were these men anyway? Were they just a bunch of stargazers, out of touch with reality? What good would gold or frankincense or myrrh be to a baby, a carpenter's son, an infant who greeted the world from an animal's feeding trough? That was reality!

But there were other realities too. Mary and Joseph had come to Bethlehem months ago to pay their taxes. Do you have money left when you pay yours? Somehow they were able to remain in Bethlehem. How did they pay for their stay? And before they could go back to Nazareth, Joseph's angel rerouted them to Egypt. Because of Herod's murderous search for the Christ child, Mary and Joseph could not return to Israel until Herod's death.

No one knows what happened to the royal gifts. But it is certain that Jesus' family was needy, and it is possible that the Magi's gifts sustained them.

We have needy people in our community too. While we don't have the privilege of offering lavish gifts to God Incarnate as he lay in the manger, we are able to give simple gifts in his name. The same writer who told us of the wise men also recorded these words of Jesus: "I tell you the truth, whatever you did for one of the least of these brothers of mine, you did for me" (Matthew 25:40). Next we're going to assemble some gifts we hope will meet the needs of [*name the agency*]. [*Introduce the art director who will be overseeing the gift project (or continue if you have assumed that role as well); begin work on gift bags.*]

Conclusion

[*After finishing the gift bags and cleaning up, introduce the family or families who will deliver them. Send them out with a blessing, and pronounce a benediction over all who worked to give in Jesus' name:*] We ask your blessing, Lord, upon those who give and those who receive these simple gifts. Meet the needs of our homes and hearts we pray. Amen.

Magi-cal Moments Drama

CAST

Narrator: a good reader who will privately rehearse the passages before the day of the event; will meet with actors (perhaps just before the event begins) to review the scenes they will act out

Prophet: a reader with a deep voice, possibly a grandfather—; appears in scene 2

Three Magi: carry gifts representing gold, incense, or myrrh; may wear robes—; appear in scenes 1, 3, 4

King Herod: wears a crown; may wear a robe—; appears in scenes 2, 3

Mary, Joseph, child: may wear robes—; appear in scene 4

Star-child: holds a large construction-paper star pasted at the end of a cardboard tube—; appears in scenes 1, 3, 4

[*King Herod enters and sits in front-row seat reserved for him. Prophet and Mary, Joseph, and child may enter behind Magi and quietly take their places at back of room.*]

SCENE 1

NARRATOR: After Jesus was born in Bethlehem in Judea, during the time of King Herod [*gesture with hand toward King Herod*], Magi from the east came to Jerusalem and asked, "Where is the one who has been born king of the Jews? We saw his star in the east and have come to worship him." [*As soon as Narrator stands to read, Magi enter, led by Star-child. As they pass those seated, they lean in toward the people searching for the Christ child. Upon arriving at front, Star-child and Magi "freeze" for scene 2.*]

SCENE 2

NARRATOR: When King Herod heard this he was disturbed [*King Herod rises, paces in front of first row*], and all Jerusalem [*King Herod points to seated assembly*] with him. When he had called together all the people's chief priests and teachers of the law [*King Herod points to clergy and lawyers who may be present*] he asked them where the Christ was to be born. "In Bethlehem in Judea," they replied, "for this is what the prophet has written:

PROPHET: "'But you, Bethlehem, in the land of Judah, are by no means least among the rulers of Judah; for out of you will come a ruler who will be the shepherd of my people Israel.'"

SCENE 3

NARRATOR: Then Herod called the Magi secretly [*King Herod turns toward Magi, who unfreeze, and creeps toward them, "whispering" his question furtively; Magi nod in understanding*] and found out from them the exact time the star had appeared. He sent them to Bethlehem [*Herod points to back of room*] and said, "Go and make a careful search for the child. As soon as you find him, report to me, so that I too may go and worship him." [*Herod watches Magi go.*] After they had heard the king, they went on their way, and the star they had seen in the east went ahead of them until it stopped over the place where the child was.

[*To the assembly:*] As the Star-child leads the Magi, quietly and quickly turn your chairs so they face the other end of the room. [*When most have settled in their turned seats, Star-child slowly leads Magi toward Mary, Joseph, and child.*]

SCENE 4

NARRATOR: When they saw the star, they were over-joyed. On coming to the house, they saw the child with his mother Mary, and they bowed down and worshiped him. [*Magi kneel reverently.*] Then they opened their treasures and presented him with gifts of gold and of incense and of myrrh. [*Brief silence*] And having been warned in a dream not to go back to Herod, they returned to their country by another route.* [*Magi exit room; Star-child sits, laying star on floor.*]

---

* Narrator's and prophet's lines are from Matthew 2:1–12.

Magi-cal Moments

Responsibilities

• *Confirm the project with the agency of choice.* Select the agency you wish to help and interview its leader. Ask about specific needs; discuss number of gift bags desired; arrange a time convenient for their delivery after the event.

Ideas: students in before- or after-school programs can use pencils, erasers, notebooks, crayons, and granola bars; seniors at a care facility might enjoy stamped postcards, pens, tissue packs, and bookmarks; women at a shelter would appreciate personal care items (sample sizes are fine).

• *Solicit donations.* Let your congregation know what is needed and where and when donations will be collected. The gift bag contents won't need to be the same in each, so you can accept all items given.

Supplies

• brown lunch bags

• pencils, markers

• crown and star patterns (see page 31) cut from cardboard for easy tracing

• construction paper, scissors, glue or glue sticks

• assorted star stickers, glitter, sequins, flat-back "jewels," buttons, etc.

• staplers

• donations collected from congregation

Preparation

• Set up work tables; put signs on them to designate their use ("Sort donations," "Decorate bags," "Fill bags," etc.).

• Place supplies where they are needed.

Directions

Be prepared to guide this activity. Announce directions clearly. Help families choose the task they are best suited for. Troubleshoot questions that arise.

For Sorters

• From donations collected, put similar items together.

• Make a miscellaneous pile for one-of-a-kind items.

For Crafters

• Choose a star or crown theme.

• Select brown bag and other supplies, including pattern, if you decide to use one.

• Decorate one side of each bag only; leave plain fold-over space at top.

For Stuffers

• Collect decorated bags as they are finished.

• Insert items common to every bag first.

• Add one-of-a-kind items last.

• Fold top to back and staple.

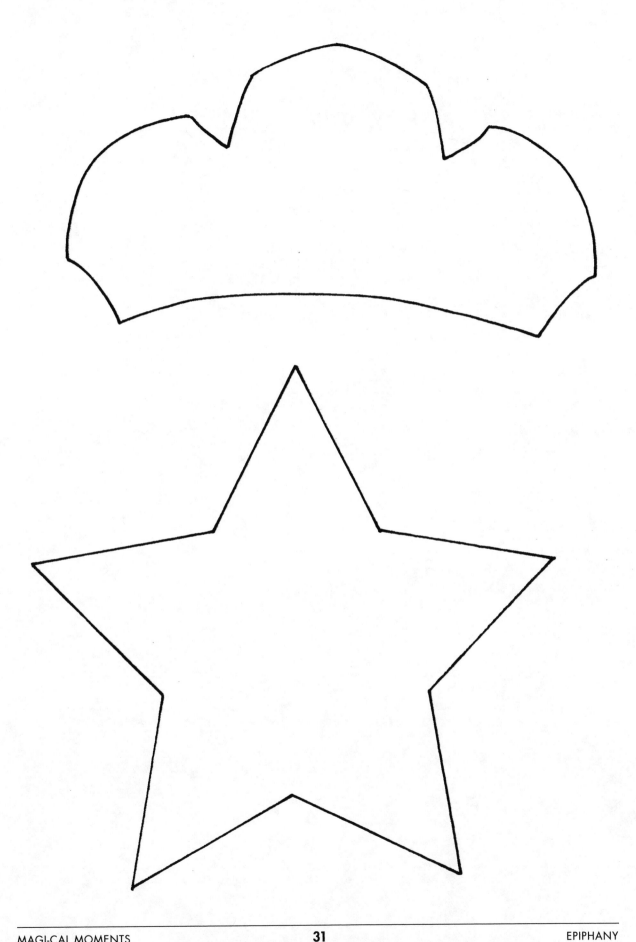

CHAPTER 4

Cross Words

LENT

Just as Moses lifted up the snake in the desert, so the Son of Man must be lifted up, that everyone who believes in him may have eternal life.

JOHN 3:15

Lent is the most ancient of the liturgical seasons. In the early days of the Church, those who had chosen to embrace the Christian faith embarked on forty days of fasting and penitence, following the example of Jesus himself. They studied the Scriptures, looked deeply into their hearts, and promised to fashion their lives anew according to the gospel.

For the ancient Christians, and for us, Lent—from the Latin word for "springtime"—is a time of renewal and rededication. In the seasonal Scripture readings, we walk the way of the cross with Jesus, looking forward to rising with him to new life.

The often-puzzling story of our Lord's passion is represented in this home activity that prepares us for the Sundays of Lent. With the help of take-home pages available at church each Sunday, everyday places—the refrigerator door, the dinner table—are transformed into spiritual spaces where we contemplate the mystery of God's saving work.

Cross Words

This series of interactive devotionals should be completed at home. The church will distribute the pages weekly. Notice that each page is used during the week *preceding* the stated Sunday.

The first distribution (the last Sunday of Epiphany) includes two sheets: the crossword grid and general instructions (copied back-to-back) and the page for Lent 1. On Lent 1 the page for Lent 2 is given out, and so forth through Lent 5, when the final page (for Lent 6—Palm/Passion Sunday) is distributed. Keep extra pages on hand for those who may miss a week or begin late.

You may want to post an enlarged puzzle to fill in gradually or use as an all-church activity during Holy Week.

Announce your plan in the church bulletin beginning late in Epiphany, as well as where the pages can be found each week.

Solution to **CROSS WORDS**

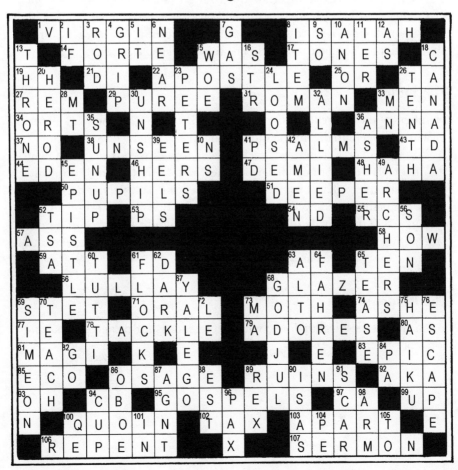

How to Use the Cross Words Activity Pages

Each Sunday you will be able to pick up a new page to use the following week. You will keep this page posted (other side showing) on the refrigerator, and place new pages next to it in succession. The pages will contain 4 parts:

The Bible

This section will list the Scripture passages you should read during the week in preparation for the next Sunday. Look at these passages in a variety of ways. Explore them in different translations. Read them silently or aloud, alone or with others. Find them in storybooks in the children's section of a library. Retell the narratives—write them, act them out, question them, compare them.

The Puzzle

New clues will be listed every week to help you solve the crossword. Some clues have been designed especially for younger family members—give them first chance at solving them. Clues in *italic* are hymn texts; clues in "quotation marks" are from Scripture. Most 2-letter (and some 3-letter) solutions are abbreviations. Use a pencil to fill in answers, and keep a good eraser nearby.

The Table

Members of the household choose when and where to eat the week's special meal together. Fill in the information on the week's activity page as a reminder.

You will create a centerpiece each week in a shallow box or basket, which should be placed on or near the meal table. Select items (or words or pictures) for the centerpiece that connect with the Bible texts. The activity page will list ideas, but participants should add to them—everyone can contribute. If a special meal will be outside of your home—at a friend's house or in a restaurant—bring the objects along. The centerpiece contents become conversation starters at the special meal.

The Response

Often the special meal dialogue will generate ideas for projects, gifts, study, song, or prayer.

W
C R O S S
R
D
S

Preparation for Lent 1

The Bible

- The temptation of Adam—Genesis 2–3; Romans 5

- The temptation of Jesus—Mark 1; Luke 4

The Puzzle

ACROSS

14. musically loud
15. used to be
17. strengthens
21. princess's nickname
22. disciple of Jesus
25. partner of *either*
26. symbol, tantalum
27. abbreviated sleeping phase
44. first garden (Genesis 2)
73. rust co-corrupter (Matthew 6)

DOWN

3. Aaron's budded (Hebrews 9)
4. stagehand
5. singular pronoun
7. fuel for car and home
8. social page article
9. strikeout
10. soon
63. male or female chorister
69. Nunc Dimittis speaker
70. instruct

The Table

This week's special meal will be

Day: _____

Time: _____

Place: _____

Add your centerpiece ideas to these: apple, fig,

The Response

We will do: _____

We will give: _____

We will think about: _____

We can sing: "Forty Days and Forty Nights"

We will pray for: _____

Preparation for Lent 2

The Bible

• Abraham gives up his son, Isaac—Genesis 22

• God gives up his Son, Jesus—John 3

The Puzzle

ACROSS

33. "The grace of God that brings salvation has appeared to all ___" (Titus 2:11)
34. meal leftovers
36. Jerusalem prophetess (Luke 2)
37. opposite of yes
41. many of King David's hymns
43. end zone score
46. not his
47. prefix meaning half
48. laughing syllables
50. students

DOWN

11. comparative ending
12. ancient Roman copper coin
15. *From deepest ___ I cry to thee*
16. airport code for Stuttgart, Germany
18. United States' northern neighbor
20. called a fox by Jesus (Luke 13)
26. tithe
30. offload boat cargo
32. working together (with)
33. L and O connections
35. first light of day
56. God gave the world his one and only ___ (John 3:16)

The Table

This week's special meal will be

Day: _____

Time: _____

Place: _____

Add your centerpiece ideas to these: bundle of twigs, toy lamb,

The Response

We will do: _____

We will give: _____

We will think about: _____

We can sing: "What Wondrous Love Is This"

We will pray for: _____

Preparation for Lent 3

The Bible

• Moses gets water—Exodus 17

• Jesus is the Living Water—John 4

The Puzzle

ACROSS

29. pulpy veggies
38. *O God, ___, yet ever near*
51. more profound
52. sang Little Teapot, "Just ___ me over and pour"
53. correspondence afterthought
54. Fargo's state
55. some Sisters
58. ___ do you do?
59. envelope heads-up
66. *Lully, ___, thou little tiny child*

DOWN

36. tribe of Israel (Genesis 49)
39. snakelike fish
40. compass points
41. law enforcement agency
42. sometimes sevenfold
45. New Testament letter
49. bow and arrow users (Genesis 49:23)
52. retirement account
60. ___-frutti
64. *-heit* starter
67. Eli's cheer

The Table

This week's special meal will be

Day: _____

Time: _____

Place: _____

Add your centerpiece ideas to these: shell, rock,

The Response

We will do: _____

We will give: _____

We will think about: _____

We can sing: "Guide Me, O Thou Great Jehovah"

We will pray for: _____

Preparation for Lent 4

The Bible

• The blind see—John 9

• The hungry are fed—John 6

• The lost is found—Luke 15

The Puzzle

ACROSS

61. R _ _ or _ _R
63. branch of the military
65. number of commandments given
Moses (Exodus 20)
68. potter, sometimes
69. cancels delete
71. unwritten, as in tradition
74. Arthur's tennis stadium
77. that is
79. is devoted to
80. ___ *longs the deer for cooling streams*

DOWN

6. close
61. what shepherds watched
68. Christmas greeting, in Uppsala
72. in sol-fa, A-flat but not G-sharp
73. Pa's wife
75. 17-syllable poetic form
76. "How shall we ___ if we ignore
such a great salvation?"
(Hebrews 2:3)
82. Ready! Set! ___!
78. sports equipment
84. Ma's husband
86. double-reed instrument

The Table

This week's special meal will be

Day: _____

Time: _____

Place: _____

Add your centerpiece ideas here: sunglasses, can of soup,

The Response

We will do: _____

We will give: _____

We will think about: _____

We can sing: "O, for a Thousand Tongues to Sing"

We will pray for: _____

Preparation for Lent 5

The Bible

• Dead bones are restored to life—Ezekiel 37

• Lazarus is restored to life—John 11

• Seeds die to give life—John 12

The Puzzle

ACROSS

1. Mary, the mother of Jesus
8. prophet, son of Amoz
19. initials of hymn tune "Michael" composer
81. wise men (Matthew 2)
83. heroic poem or novel
85. -*logical* beginning
86. inedible orangelike fruit
89. ancient archaeological remains (Isaiah 58:12)
92. sometimes goes by
93. exclamation of surprise or fear
94. public radio?

DOWN

2. perchance
87. rep.
88. Atlantic coast winter hours
89. Tyrannosaurus ___
90. it ___ ___ if
91. mark of healing
94. "May this ___ be taken from me" (Matthew 26:39)
96. kiss of peace
100. with D, Latin proof
101. hotel homophone

The Table

This week's special meal will be

Day: _____

Time: _____

Place: _____

Add your centerpiece ideas to these: bone, wheat,

The Response

We will do: _____

We will give: _____

We will think about: _____

We can sing: "Immortal, Invisible"

We will pray for: _____

Preparation for Lent 6
(Palm/Passion Sunday)

The Bible

• Isaiah calls for salvation—Isaiah 45

• Jesus makes salvation possible—Luke 23

The Puzzle

ACROSS

31. Pilate's government (John 18)
57. *ox and ___ before him bow*
95. Matthew, Mark, Luke, and John
97. between NA and SA
99. beverage, with 7-
100. cornerstone
102. Matthew collected it
103. not together
106. "Unless you ___, you too will all perish" (Luke 13:3)
107. homily

DOWN

13. *the Father, on his sapphire ___*
23. whose denial the cock crow signaled
24. ___ *from Pharaoh's bitter yoke*
28. ___ of Olives, place of prayer (Luke 22)
62. *Go to ___ Gethsemane*
65. mock (Luke 23)
98. "To whom has the ___ of the LORD been revealed?" (Isaiah 53:1)
104. school fitness class
105. ___ *God be the glory*

The Table

This week's special meal will be

Day: _____

Time: _____

Place: _____

Add your centerpiece ideas to these: 1 AM blocks, cross,

The Response

We will do: _____

We will give: _____

We will think about: _____

We can sing: "At the Name of Jesus"

We will pray for: _____

CHAPTER 5

Surprises

EASTERTIDE

*He was taken up before their very eyes,
and a cloud hid him from their sight.*

ACTS 1:9

Christ is risen indeed! Easter Sunday—and the weeks of Eastertide that follow—are the most joyful days in the Church year, as Christians around the world celebrate the resurrection of Jesus Christ and his ascension into heaven. For Christians, Easter is a season of heartfelt alleluias!

When the community of faith arrives at church, we'll treat them to an unexpected celebration of Christ's resurrection, ascension, and promised return. We can't reveal all about this indoor/outdoor activity, except that Holy Scripture, musical prayer, simple breakfast fare, interactive place mats, and bright balloons are included.

Name the Surprise . . .

Write your answers between the lines. Or color the balloons. Or do both!

This natural phenomenon occurred when the angel rolled away the stone:

The angel said these words to the women at the tomb:

The women encountered this person as they left the tomb:

The soldiers told this lie about Jesus:

This mysterious person traveled to Emmaus:

Jesus' instructed his disciples to:

The disciples thought they saw this in a Jerusalem room:

This mysterious entry frightened the disciples:

The disciples ate this unexpected breakfast on the seashore:

Jesus and Peter spoke about these animals:

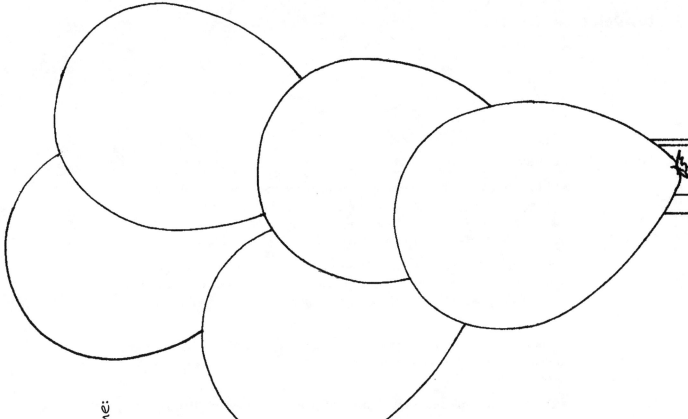

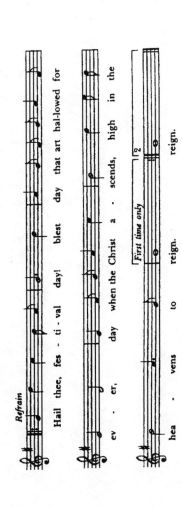

Refrain

Hail thee, fes - ti - val day! blest day that art hal-lowed for

ev - er, day when the Christ a - scends, high in the

First time only

hea - vens to reign. reign.

Surprises

Preparation

• Include as few people as possible in the preparations for this unannounced activity. Those who normally have responsibilities during your church's education hour are good candidates. They'll appreciate being informed of the change and will be glad to help.

• Plan a time for a light breakfast. This should require minimal preparation and may include individual boxes of cereal, pitchers of milk, diced fruit in paper cups, plastic spoons, and napkins. You'll know if coffee is optional for your congregation.

• Make placemats: Set machine to enlarge at 129%. Copy onto 11" x 17" paper. Put at the tables. Place crayons on all tables. (See answers to place mat questions below.)

• Rent a helium tank and buy helium-grade balloons. Fill the balloons and tape them around the breakfast area within reach of adults. You will need at least one balloon per family unit (parents with children, couples, singles). Make sure you don't fill the balloons too early; you can determine how long the balloons will stay inflated by checking the balloon package or by doing a trial run the day before.

• Place trash containers where they can be easily accessed.

Answers to Place Mat Questions

(1) Earthquake (Matthew 28:2); (2) "He is risen" (Mark 16:6); (3) Jesus (Matthew 28:9); (4) "His disciples came during the night and stole him away while we were asleep" (Matthew 28:13); (5) Jesus (Luke 24:13ff.); (6) Go, baptize, teach (Matthew 28:19–20); (7) a ghost (Luke 24:37); (8) Jesus appeared in a locked room (John 20:26); (9) bread and fish prepared by Jesus (John 21:13); (10) lambs, sheep (John 21:15ff.)

The Spiritual Menu

• Assign volunteers to direct people to the breakfast room.

• The refrain of "Hail Thee, Festival Day" (printed on place mats) should be used as a blessing before the meal and a benediction following it.

• Review the events on the place mat. Ask the participants to imagine they live in Jerusalem at the time of the crucifixion—surprising times. The people of Jerusalem had received many shocks in the last several months. Let the diners respond with their answers to the place mat questions as you reprise the biblical narratives that describe these days.

• One more surprise: Explain that the breakfast will conclude outside. Each family or group will take a balloon from the room. Silence must be kept from the time they step outside to the moment they reenter the church. Tell them to listen to what you say and watch what you do—they will release their balloons on your signal.

Wait until all are outside. Holding a balloon in your hand, say: "Luke writes these words about Jesus and the apostles:

"After his suffering, he showed himself to these men and gave many convincing proofs that he was alive. He appeared to them over a period of forty days and spoke about the kingdom of God. On one occasion, while he was eating with them, he gave them this command: 'Do not leave Jerusalem, but wait for the gift my Father promised, which you have heard me speak about. For John baptized with water, but in a few days you will be baptized with the Holy Spirit. . . .

"'I am going to send you what my Father has promised; but stay in the city until you have been clothed with power from on high.'

"When he had led them out to the vicinity of Bethany, he lifted up his hands and blessed them. While he was blessing them, he left them and was taken up into heaven. . . .

"He was taken up before their very eyes, and a cloud hid him from their sight."

Release your balloon, and without comment nod to the people to do the same. After a moment, continue reading:

"They were looking intently up into the sky as he was going, when suddenly two men dressed in white stood beside them. 'Men of Galilee,' they said, 'why do you stand here looking into the sky? This same Jesus, who has been taken from you into heaven, will come back in the same way you have seen him go into heaven.'"

Repeat the verse joyfully:

"This same Jesus, who has been taken from you into heaven, will come back in the same way you have seen him go into heaven."

Lead the people toward the church door. Stop in front of it, concluding:

"Then they worshiped him and returned to Jerusalem with great joy. And they stayed continually at the temple, praising God."*

---

* Scripture quoted from Acts 1:3–5; Luke 24:49–51; Acts 1:9–11; Luke 24:52–53.

CHAPTER 6

Happy Birthday!
PENTECOST

*"You will receive the gift of the Holy Spirit.
The promise is for you and your children."*

ACTS 2:38–39

It's a birthday party! On Pentecost Sunday—50 days after Easter—Christians celebrate the birth of the Church 2,000 years ago in the crowded city of Jerusalem. Huddled and afraid in an upper room, the apostles and others gathered were filled with the Holy Spirit and inspired to go out into the world and preach the good news. Today and throughout the season of Pentecost, the Church celebrates their courage and their joy—and the amazing work of the Spirit.

Everyone can prepare and participate in this interactive celebration of Pentecost, the birthday of the Church. From the items you will bring in response to the requests in the church bulletin, centers will be designed where you can explore other languages, experience Babel, remember your baptism, illustrate the Trinity, and search hymn texts. We will conclude with a birthday party for the Church.

Happy Birthday

This Pentecost anniversary event requires every generation of the congregation to assist with preparation as well as celebration. By exploring languages, reconstructing Babel, remembering baptism, diagramming the Trinity, and searching hymn text, they will better understand the events recorded by Luke in the second chapter of Acts. You are likely to find that their involvement prior to the event will motivate many to attend. The birthday party for the church is a fitting conclusion for the evening.

You may want to schedule these activities for the evening of Pentecost or an evening between Pentecost and Trinity Sunday, setting aside 2 hours for the proceedings. As in the previous intergenerational activities, the youngest participant should be at least 5 years old, and groups should consist of 4 to 6 people representing 2 to 4 generations. These "family" groups will move together throughout the evening.

Choose 6 center facilitators and assign them responsibility for 1 of the centers. Each facilitator will prepare, introduce, and monitor her or his center's activity. The following pages contain worksheets and patterns to help each center facilitator. Meet with these facilitators 3 to 4 weeks before the activity date. At that time it would be a good idea to put the following items on your agenda:

• Give each facilitator page(s) for her or his activity.

• Read the pages together and discuss resources and budget.

• Review deadlines for bulletin announcements, which will describe the event and list raw materials needed and volunteers' tasks.

• Choose the room or area for each center.

• Remind facilitators that the groups will move from center to center throughout the evening. At the designated time, the groups will converge in a central location for the birthday party.

"Other Tongues" Bibles

Preparation

Borrow as many foreign-language Bibles as possible. Good sources include families with immigrant forebears, libraries (public, parochial), missionaries, foreign-language departments at schools, and exchange students. Arrange for collection and return with each donor. Explain how the Bibles will be labeled and used. Enclose a brief note of thanks with each when you restore it to its owner.

To label each Bible with the name of its owner and the language represented, you will need adding machine paper, a fine-tip marker, and tape. Cut a piece of paper a little longer than twice the height of the book. Print the information in the middle. Wrap around the book's front cover, taping paper together inside (do not tape the book itself). Also display a large-print English-language Bible open to Acts 2:14–47.

Introducing the Activity

"On the day of Pentecost, as recorded in the second chapter of Acts, crowds from Mesopotamia, Judea, Cappadocia, Pontus, Asia, Phrygia, Pamphylia, Egypt, Rome, Crete, and elsewhere heard their own languages coming from the mouths of the Galileans. They were bewildered, amazed, perplexed; they asked questions; they offered answers; they made accusations. Finally, the apostle Peter stood up and explained what was going on. You can read his words in Acts 2, verses 14 to the end. [*Point to Bible open to this passage.*] Today, because of the efforts of Bible translators and distributors, the Word of God is available to people around the world in their own language. We have some of these Bibles here for you to see.

"These have been loaned to us for this event by the people whose names are on the labels. Many different languages are represented: [*name some*]. Please choose a Bible and carefully examine it. Find your favorite Bible verse and read it to yourself in a new way."

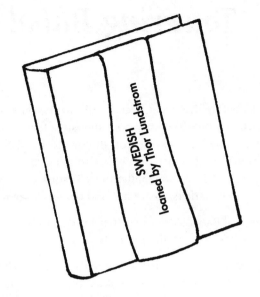

"Other Tongues" Bibles

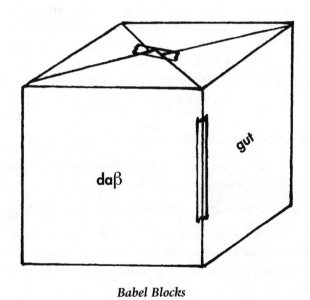

Babel Blocks

Towering Babel

Preparation

- At least 2 weeks before this event, recruit volunteers to help make the alphabet blocks. Gather about 40 empty boutique-style facial tissue boxes and as many pages from the business section of your local newspaper (these are desirable for their small print). You will also need miscellaneous scraps of cardboard or poster board (no smaller than 5″ square). Supply your helpers with broad-tip black markers, clear tape, and copies of the instructions.

- Locate the tower of Babel story as written for children. The length of a children's version will fit this activity perfectly.

- Be sure the area you designate for this activity is free of chairs and tables. If you have story rugs in your education area, this would be a perfect time to borrow them.

- Before the first participants arrive, build a tower with the finished blocks, and place the story/book at its base.

Introducing the Activity

Appoint someone in the group to read the story. When participants are settled, signal the reader to begin. When the reader is finished, invite participants to topple the tower and then examine the letters and words on the blocks. Ask, "What do you notice about the words or letters on the blocks?" [*Allow response.*]

"At Babel's destruction, the languages of confusion were born. How did that change on the day of Pentecost?" [*Allow response.*]

When discussion ends, ask the group to rebuild the tower for those who will come next.

Instructions for Creating the Blocks

- On scrap cardboard, trace the open side of the box. Cut out the cardboard; tape the cardboard square over the hole.

- Wrap the box in a newspaper page. Tape the blocks at a side edge and at the ends (box top and bottom).

- Using a broad black marker, print a foreign letter (Greek, Arabic, Russian, etc.) or short word (French, German, Spanish, etc.) on each of the 4 sides of the blocks.

- Return finished blocks to church by [date] and leave them in [place].

Baptism Mural

Preparation

• Choose a wall where this mural can be assembled and seen easily. Newspapers and other printing companies may donate end rolls of paper if you ask. Shelf or kraft paper can also be used. Attach the mural background to the wall before the activity begins.

• Photocopy shell pattern (see page 58) on assorted pastel paper.

• Arrange work tables and chairs near the mural. You will also need scissors, fine-tip markers, glue sticks, and shell patterns.

Introducing the Activity

"When the anxious crowd asked Peter, 'What shall we do?' in response to the extraordinary events of the day of Pentecost, he answered, 'Repent and be baptized, every one of you, in the name of Jesus Christ for the forgiveness of your sins' (Acts 2:38).

"The shell is a common symbol representing the act of baptism. Every one of you who has been baptized may cut out a shell (representing your baptism), print your name and birth date on it, and glue it to this wall mural. Your efforts will remain on display through next Sunday as a witness to our church community's obedience through baptism."

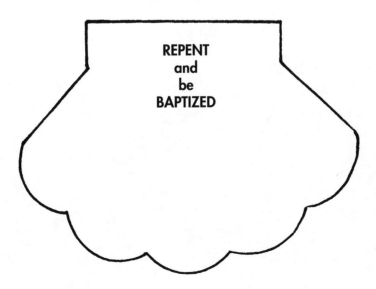

REPENT
and
be
BAPTIZED

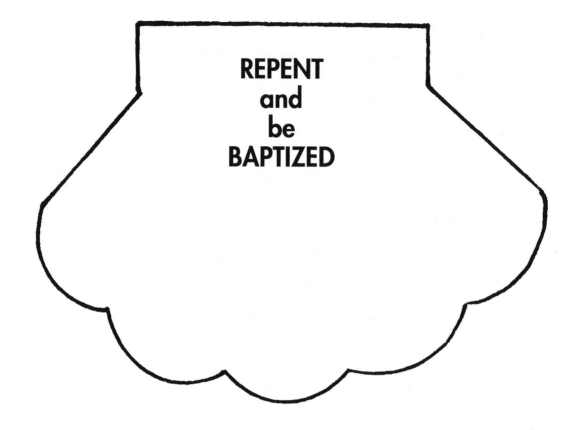

REPENT
and
be
BAPTIZED

Trinity Symbol

Supplies

Each symbol requires 2 pieces of construction paper and 4 circle stickers. You will also need scissors, 12″ rulers, fine-tip (dark) markers, and school glue.

Preparation

• Make copies of the instructions and pattern for each artist.

• Construct a sample symbol to show participants.

• Set up work spaces (tables and chairs) and supplies table.

Introducing the Activity

"At Pentecost the promised Holy Spirit made an unforgettable appearance. From that day forward, God in all his fullness—Father, Son, Holy Spirit—was manifest to the Church.

"This three-in-one paradox has been symbolized in many ways. You'll create a diagram of the Trinity following the instructions provided. [*Show sample.*]

[*As people work, explain conversationally how the diagram reads.*] "God is one [*see center*]. The Father is God; the Son is God; the Holy Spirit is God. [*See lines connecting to center.*] But the Son is neither the Father nor the Holy Spirit; the Father is neither the Holy Spirit nor the Son; the Holy Spirit is neither the Son nor the Father."

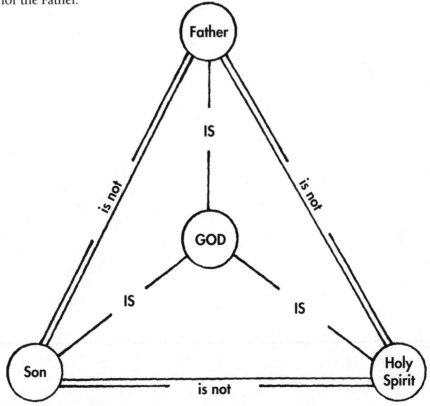

Instructions for Creating the Trinity Symbol

- Choose 2 pieces of construction paper. From one, cut out the triangle. Glue it to the center of the other piece of paper.

- Choose 4 stickers. Press one in the triangle's center. Press one at each point of the triangle.

- Print "God," "Father," "Son," and "Holy Spirit" inside the circles (see facilitator's sample).

- Using a ruler, draw connecting lines from "God" to each point of the triangle. Label all lines (see diagram).

- Explain your symbol to others in the group.

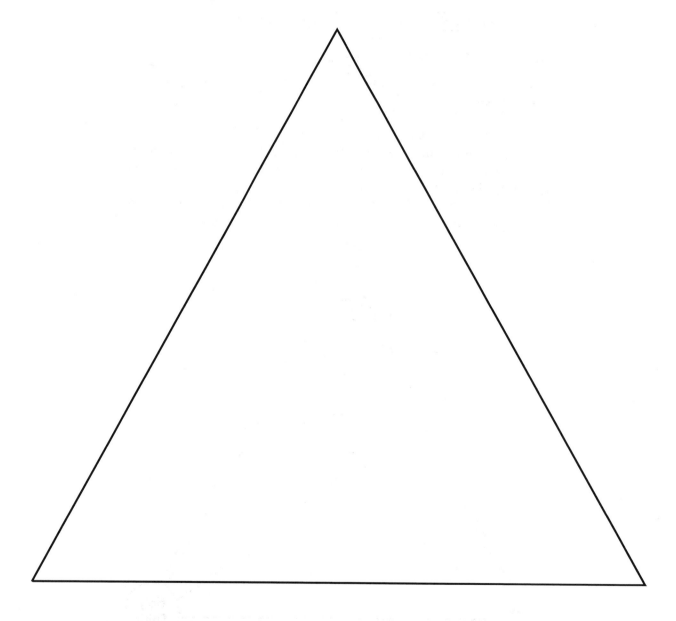

Stanza Search

Preparation

• Collect a variety of hymnals containing Pentecost hymns. (Or, if your church owns a copy license for your pew hymnal, make copies of at least 3 different Pentecost hymns.)

• Make enough copies of the search sheet for each participant.

• Assemble and sharpen pencils.

• Set up tables and chairs, preferably in a room with a piano.

Introducing the Activity

[*Make sure every person (including children) has a hymnal or copies of the hymns, search sheet, and pencil.*] "We're going to search for Pentecost words and ideas in some of our hymns. You may choose one hymn for your whole group to examine, or each of you may work with a different hymn. You have been given a stanza search sheet that will help you. Do the searches that most interest you. For example, make a list of words in the hymn that describe wind or fire or language, or make a list of words that are used more than once. As a group, read the suggestions given on the search sheet before you begin.

"Go ahead and make notes on your search sheet. After a few minutes, discuss your discoveries together. You may prefer to work in twos; that's fine. Feel free to sing and use the piano if you wish. You'll have about 15 minutes to work."

Stanza Search Sheet

What words in the hymn describe or hint at wind? Fire? Language?

Does the hymn contain a prayer? A personal challenge?

What activities are assigned to the Holy Spirit?

Are any words or phrases repeated? Are any unclear to you?

Which phrases in the text compare to those in Acts 2?

What would you include if you were to draw a picture of these hymn stanzas?

Birthday Party

Preparation

- Ask some members of the congregation to contribute iced cupcakes, to be delivered Pentecost Sunday morning. Keep a tally of each dozen promised and compare it to the number of expected participants. Allow for extras.

- Arrange for the setup of tables and chairs. Decorate simply, perhaps using candles (fire), balloons (wind), and doves.

- Set out small plates, napkins, forks, cups, milk, and serving pitchers.

- Recruit servers and a cleanup crew.

- Coordinate the concluding activity with the clergyperson who will lead it. Provide that person with the following remarks.

Party Blessing

"Today we celebrate the birthday of the Church, the day of the coming of the Holy Spirit to be our Guide and Comforter. Listen to Acts 2:42–47:

> "They devoted themselves to the apostles' teaching and to the fellowship, to the breaking of bread and to prayer. Everyone was filled with awe, and many wonders and miraculous signs were done by the apostles. All the believers were together and had everything in common. Selling their possessions and goods, they gave to anyone as he had need. Every day they continued to meet together in the temple courts. They broke bread in their homes and ate together with glad and sincere hearts, praising God and enjoying the favor of all the people. And the Lord added to their number daily those who were being saved."

"Let us also continue to meet together in the temple courts here at [*say the name of your church*]. And now we eat together, with glad and thankful hearts. Let us pray. [*Pause.*] For your eternal provision for us we thank you, Father, Son, and Holy Spirit. Amen."

CHAPTER 7

The Cloud of Witnesses
ORDINARY TIME

*These were all commended for their faith, yet none of them
received what had been promised. God had planned something better
for us so that only together with us would they be made perfect.
Therefore, since we are surrounded by such a great cloud of witnesses, . . .
let us fix our eyes on Jesus, the author and perfecter of our faith.*

HEBREWS 11:39–12:2

What's so ordinary about Ordinary Time? When you think about it, these weeks—between Pentecost and Advent—are pretty amazing. Over the quiet days of summer, the Church turns to the teachings of Jesus as we learn together how to make the gospel part of our ordinary lives.

With Hebrews 11, the great faith chapter, as a vehicle, we'll have an extra-ordinary time playing with color and symbol to fashion felt banner squares that remind us of the Old Testament characters known as "a cloud of witnesses." The common virtue of these women and men, who were real and ordinary—just like us—was faithfulness. Each time we hang this banner, we'll remember that we too wish to be a faithful people.

The Cloud of Witnesses

Preparation

This activity will accommodate up to 100 participants and take 1½ to 2 hours when done in church. It can also be a home activity. It requires felt (24 squares, background to which they will be sewn or glued, and a generous amount of scraps), small bottles of school glue, common (straight) pins, pencils, and 24 gallon-size plastic bags or large manila envelopes. You will also need dressmaker's scissors (they cut felt well) for each table and a few pairs of cuticle scissors.

Participants will work at tables in groups of 3 to 4, with representatives of 2 or more generations in each group. Each of these units will construct one banner square while discussing the Bible character it represents. You'll need to copy the study-instruction sheets as well as the full-size patterns for each square; you'll also need to make 24 copies of the square pattern on page 68.

Insert into each bag/envelope the following: one study-instruction sheet, the patterns that match it (including the square pattern), one felt square, glue, pins, and pencils. Print the Bible character's name on the envelope.

As a church event: Designate a supplies table. Fill it with felt scraps and more glue, pins, and pencils. Take note that the felt colors named in the instructions were specific to our samples (see several on book cover). They're colors from Kunin Felt (www.kunin-felt.com) and are available nationwide at craft stores. However, you can make your own color choices.

As a home event: Additional felt of the sizes and colors needed for the particular square must be added to each bag. Keep a list of the household that takes each character. Adapt, copy, and insert the instructions given below. Set a date and place for the return of completed squares.

Instructions

When people are settled at tables and each group has been given an envelope, review the description of the activity given at the beginning of this chapter. Then explain the procedure:

• Open your envelope. Make sure you have a study-instruction sheet, pattern pieces that match the instructions, glue, pins, pencils, and felt.

• Within your group, read aloud the name of the character(s) and the banner verse. Someone else in the group should read the statement beside the sketch. The sketch shows what the square may look like when you have finished assembling it.

• Discuss what you know or don't know about this character. Make some notes on the study-instruction sheet.

• Get scissors from the supplies table. Trim the felt square first. Return scrap edges to the supplies table.

• Decide who will cut what pieces. Each person can obtain the felt needed from the supplies table.

• Use pins to position pieces on the felt square. Glue one at a time, removing pins as you do so. Return scraps to the supplies table so others may use them.

SQUARE PATTERN

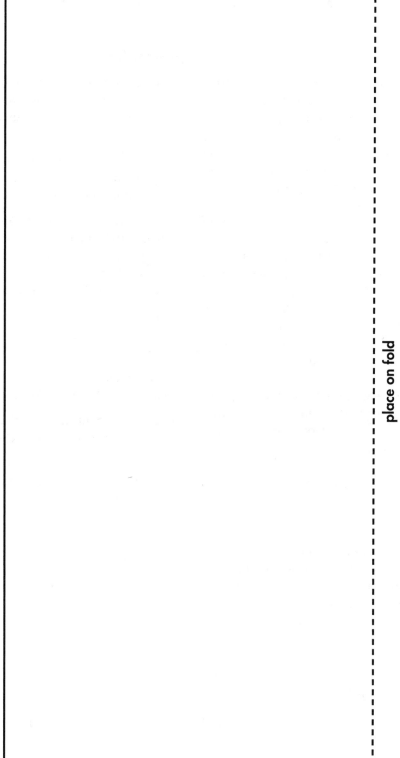

place on fold

Adam and Eve

Banner Verse: "When the woman saw that the fruit of the tree was good for food and pleasing to the eye, and also desirable for gaining wisdom, she took some and ate it. She also gave some to her husband, who was with her, and he ate it" (Genesis 3:6).

As You Work: List here and talk about words, ideas, people, and questions the characters and story bring to mind.

_____

_____

_____

_____

Supplies: patterns (square, apple, flesh, stem); felt (apple green, red, antique white, cinnamon); dressmaker's scissors; pins; glue

Instructions: Match all pattern pieces to felt and cut out. Pin stem and flesh in position at back of apple; glue. Center apple in square; glue.

*Eden's forbidden fruit was too tempting
for caretakers Adam and Eve.*

stem

flesh

apple

Enoch

Banner Verse: "Enoch walked with God; then he was no more, because God took him away" (Genesis 5:24).

As You Work: List here and talk about words, ideas, people, and questions the character and story bring to mind.

_____

_____

_____

_____

Supplies: patterns (square; small, medium, and large footprints); felt (cocoa brown; walnut, cashmere tan, apricot); dressmaker's scissors; pins; glue; yarn scrap (optional)

Instructions: Match all pattern pieces to felt and cut out. Lay yarn scrap diagonally from lower left to upper right corner of square. Place and pin footprints, with largest at bottom left, so yarn bisects each pair. Glue steps; discard yarn.

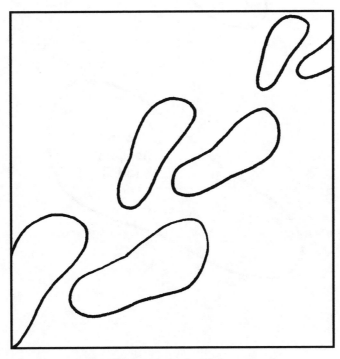

*Enoch walked with God and was no more,
for God took him away.*

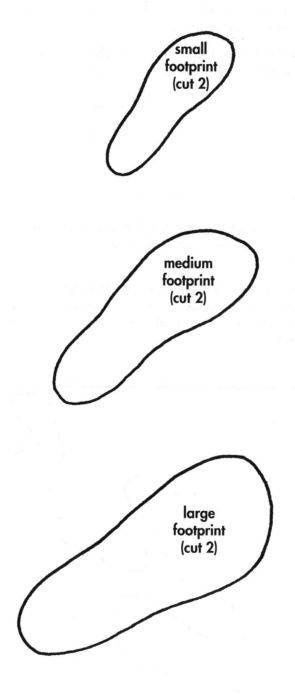

Noah

Banner Verse: "I have set my rainbow in the clouds, and it will be the sign of the covenant between me and the earth" (Genesis 9:13).

As You Work: List here and talk about words, ideas, people, and questions the character and story bring to mind.

_____

_____

_____

_____

Supplies: patterns (square; rays [7 sizes]); felt (antique white; red, orange, yellow, lime, blueberry bash, lavender, grape); dressmaker's scissors; pins; glue

Instructions: Cut out pieces in color order given above, starting with red (largest) and ending with grape (smallest). Pin rays on square. Trim curves and edges if needed. Glue; remove pins.

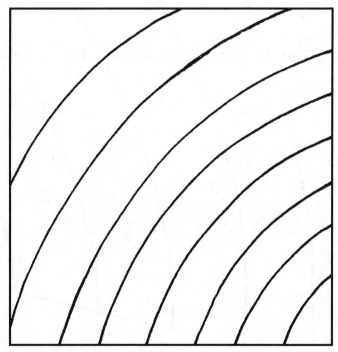

The world's first logo, designed by God himself and unveiled for Noah, is a promise of the Creator's continuing care for the earth.

NOAH—RAINBOW PATTERN

Cut rays apart to
make 7 patterns.

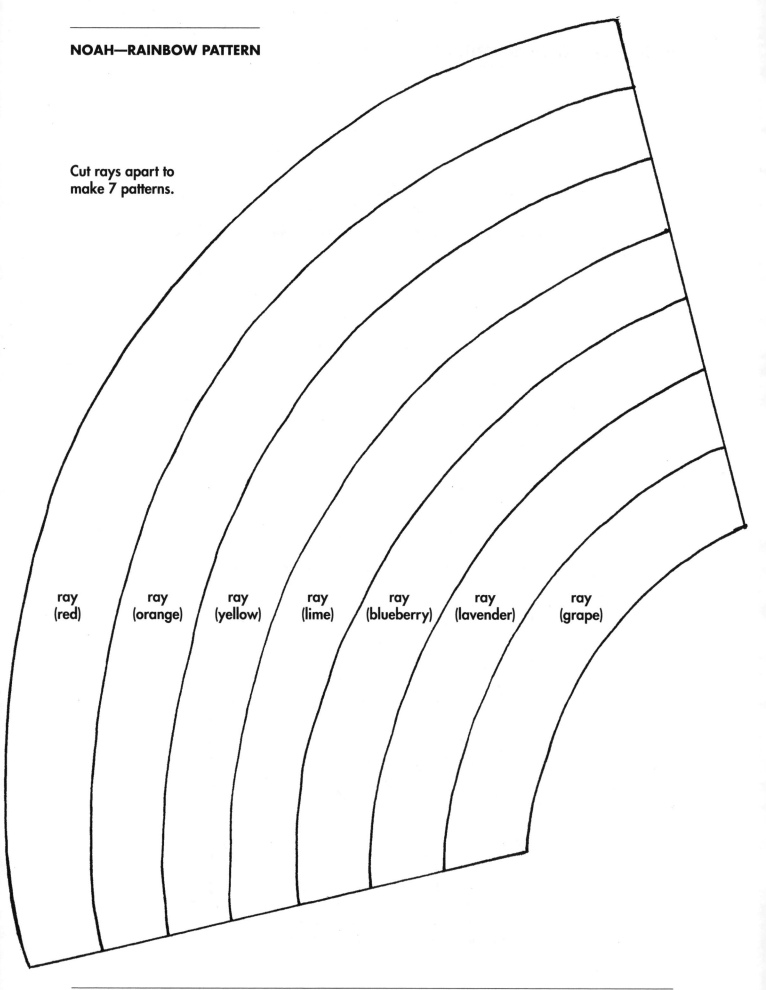

ray
(red)

ray
(orange)

ray
(yellow)

ray
(lime)

ray
(blueberry)

ray
(lavender)

ray
(grape)

Abraham

Banner Verse: "I will surely bless you and make your descendants as numerous as the stars in the sky and as the sand on the seashore" (Genesis 22:17).

As You Work: List here and talk about words, ideas, people, and questions the character and story bring to mind.

_____

_____

_____

_____

Supplies: patterns (square; under, middle, and top layers of sand; small and large stars); felt (denim; cashmere tan, butterscotch, antique white; gold); dressmaker's scissors; pins; glue

Instructions: Match all pattern pieces to felt and cut out; make extra stars if you wish. Sand layers may be glued to each other, then to the square; trim borders if needed. Set stars in sky; glue.

In terms of earth and sky, God assured Abraham's
family of his blessing upon their future.

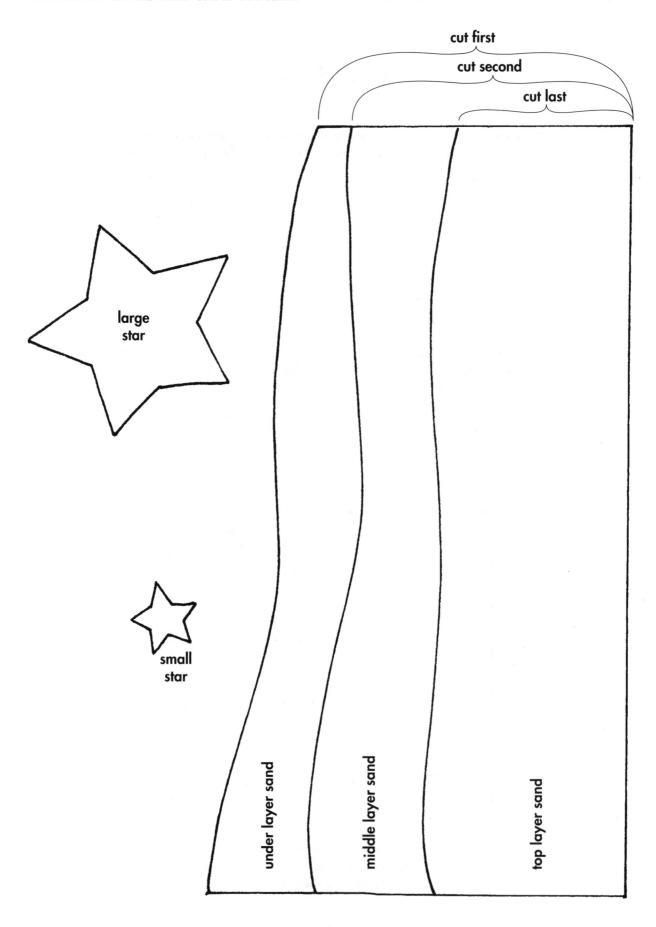

cut first

cut second

cut last

large
star

small
star

under layer sand

middle layer sand

top layer sand

Isaac

Banner Verses: "'The fire and wood are here,' Isaac said, 'but where is the lamb for the burnt offering?' . . . There in a thicket [Abraham] saw a ram caught by its horns. He went over and took the ram and sacrificed it as a burnt offering instead of his son" (Genesis 22:7b, 13b).

As You Work: List here and talk about words, ideas, people, and questions the character and story bring to mind.

_____

_____

_____

_____

Supplies: patterns (square, wool, face and ear, horn); felt (limbo lime, antique white, walnut, butterscotch); dressmaker's scissors; pins; glue

Instructions: Match all pattern pieces to felt and cut out, including slits indicated. Assemble ram by inserting horn and ear through slits; glue. Place ram in bottom left corner of square, matching straight edges; glue.

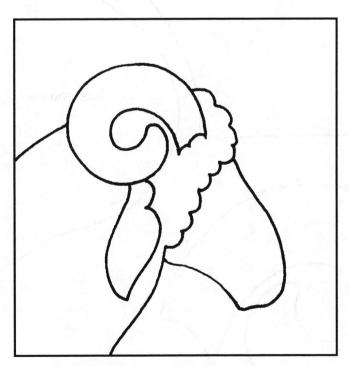

Isaac's life was spared by the ram, who foreshadowed Christ, the sacrificial Lamb of God.

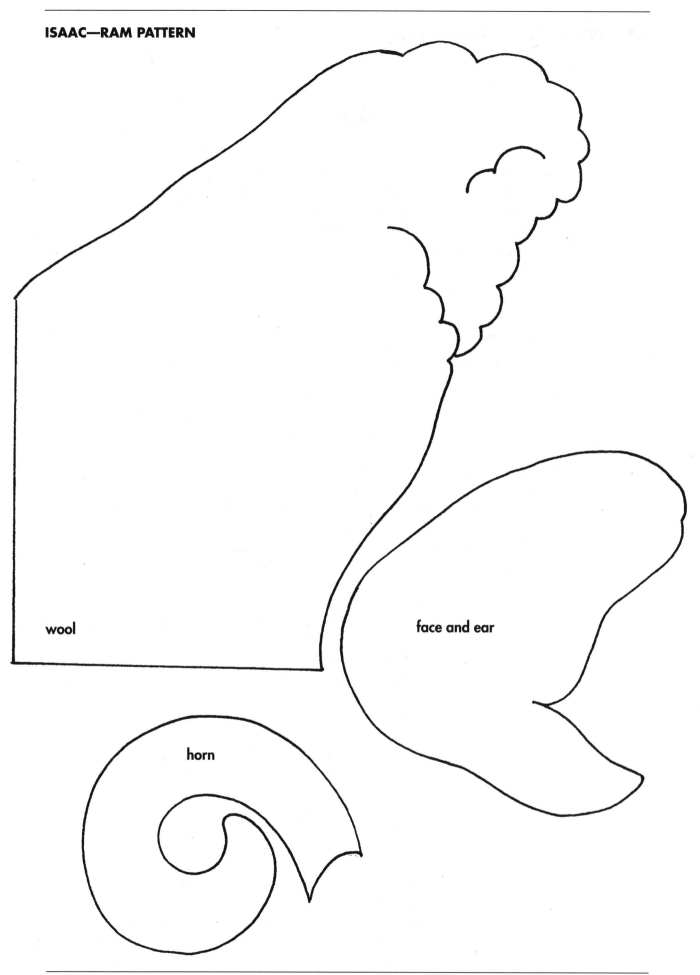

wool

face and ear

horn

Jacob

Banner Verse: "All these are the twelve tribes of Israel, and this is what their father [Jacob] said to them when he blessed them" (Genesis 49:28).

As You Work: List here and talk about words, ideas, people, and questions the character and story bring to mind.

_____

_____

_____

_____

Supplies: patterns (square; rectangle [cut 12 shades]); felt (walnut; 12 various-colored scraps); dressmaker's scissors; pins; glue

Instructions: Share the task of cutting 12 different colored rectangles from the pattern. Arrange and pin on the square; glue.

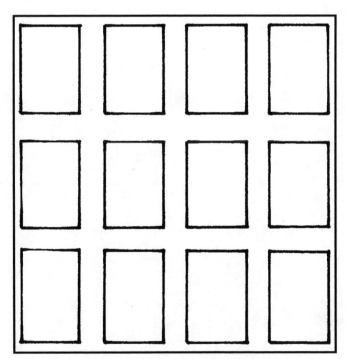

Jacob, renamed Israel by God Almighty,
gave a final blessing to each of his sons.

(cut 12)

Joseph

Banner Verse: "Now Israel loved Joseph more than any of his other sons, because he had been born to him in his old age; and he made a richly ornamented robe for him" (Genesis 37:3).

As You Work: List here and talk about words, ideas, people, and questions the character and story bring to mind.

_____

_____

_____

_____

Supplies: patterns (square; coat); felt (gray; orange, various-colored scraps); dressmaker's scissors; pins; glue

Instructions: Match coat pattern to felt and cut out. Cut narrow strips from colorful scraps; arrange on coat in your own design; glue. Trim strips that overlap coat edges. Center coat in square; glue.

This designer original belonged to a brash teenager who later became a leader of people, rescuer of family, and servant of the Lord.

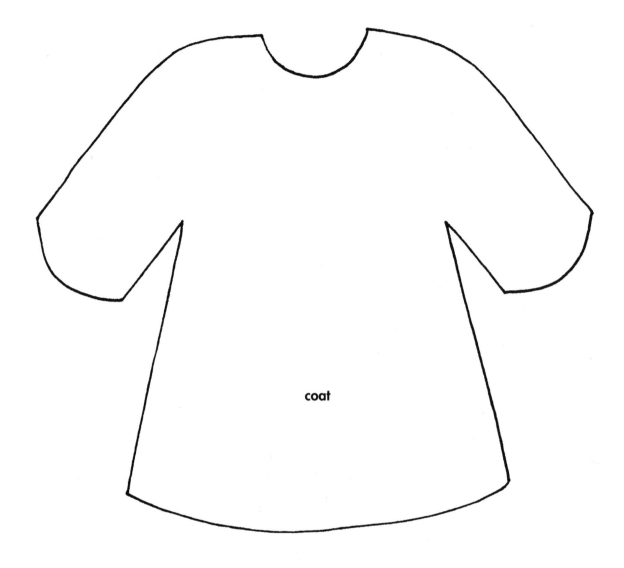

coat

(cut random width "stripes" this long in assorted colors)

Moses

Banner Verse: "There the angel of the LORD appeared to him in flames of fire from within a bush. Moses saw that though the bush was on fire it did not burn up" (Exodus 3:2).

As You Work: List here and talk about words, ideas, people, and questions the character and story bring to mind.

_____

_____

_____

_____

Supplies: patterns (square; bush; flames [3 shapes]); felt (greystone; kelly green; orange, pumpkin, red); dressmaker's scissors; pins; glue

Instructions: Match all pattern pieces to felt and cut out. Arrange flame cluster; glue to bush. Center design on square; glue.

Moses recognized that his workplace was "holy ground"
when the bush glowed with fire but was not destroyed.

Caleb

Banner Verse: "When they reached the Valley of Eschol, they cut off a branch bearing a single cluster of grapes. Two of them carried it on a pole between them" (Numbers 13:23).

As You Work: List here and talk about words, ideas, people, and questions the character and story bring to mind.

_____

_____

_____

_____

Supplies: patterns (square; cluster background; grape [cut 13]; stem with vine); felt (leaf green; lavender; orchid; teal); dressmaker's scissors; pins; glue; cuticle scissors (optional)

Instructions: Match all pattern pieces to felt and cut out. (Hints: A dime may also be used as grape pattern; vine curls cut more easily with cuticle scissors.) Glue grapes onto cluster. Place cluster and stem on square; glue.

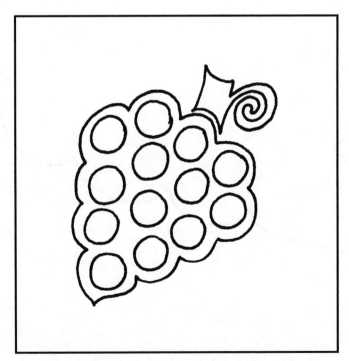

Caleb spied grape clusters so massive he had to have help carrying the evidence home.

Rahab

Banner Verse: "So she sent [the spies] away and they departed. And she tied the scarlet cord in the window" (Joshua 2:21).

As You Work: List here and talk about words, ideas, people, and questions the character and story bring to mind.

_____

_____

_____

_____

Supplies: patterns (square; interior of window; window-frame side [cut 2 of same shade]; window-frame bottom; cord); felt (harvest gold; butterscotch; french vanilla; soft beige; red); dressmaker's scissors; pins; glue

Instructions: Match all pattern pieces to felt and cut out. Assemble window; glue on frame pieces. Center window at top edge of square; glue. Place and glue red cord.

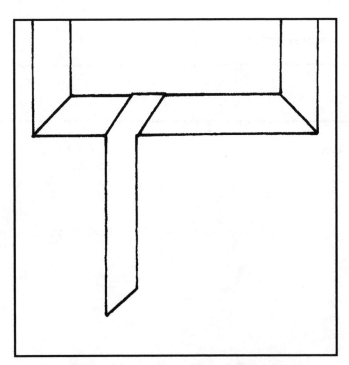

*A scarlet cord hung from her window identified
Rahab and family as friends among foes.*

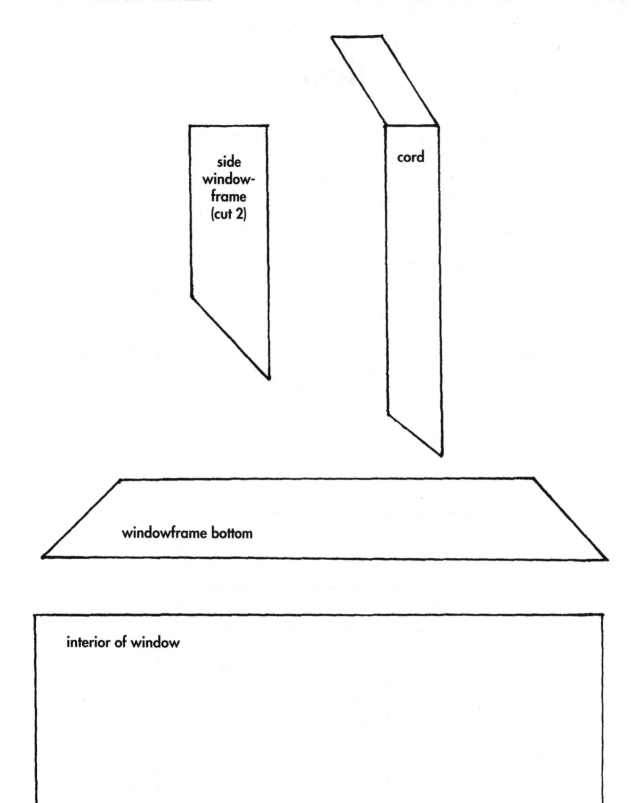

side
window-
frame
(cut 2)

cord

windowframe bottom

interior of window

Joshua

Banner Verse: "Joshua set up the twelve stones that had been in the middle of the Jordan at the spot where the priests who carried the ark of the covenant had stood" (Joshua 4:9).

As You Work: List here and talk about words, ideas, people, and questions the character and story bring to mind.

_____

_____

_____

_____

Supplies: patterns (square; sizing square); felt (hunter green; 12 various-colored scraps); dressmaker's scissors; pins; glue

Instructions: Cut out banner square. Collect scraps as large as the sizing square in a dozen colors. Cut each scrap freehand to form a stone. On banner square, pile stones, pinning each while still "building." Glue, removing pins as you go.

"When your children ask the meaning of these twelve stones, tell them!" admonished project engineer Joshua.

sizing square

**Find 12 scraps of felt,
any color. Cut into
freeform stone shapes.**

Deborah and Barak

Banner Verses: "On that day Deborah and Barak son of Abinoam sang this song: 'When the princes in Israel take the lead, when the people willingly offer themselves—praise the LORD! Hear this, you kings! Listen, you rulers! I will sing to the LORD, I will sing; I will make music to the LORD, the God of Israel'" (Judges 5:1–3).

As You Work: List here and talk about words, ideas, people, and questions the characters and story bring to mind.

_____

_____

_____

_____

Supplies: patterns (square; music notes); felt (grape; pink punch, ruby, pink mist); dressmaker's scissors; pins; glue

Instructions: Cut out pair of (eighth) notes from pattern. Cut out 3 single (quarter) notes. Position all notes on square; glue.

Judge Deborah and Captain Barak sang a victory duet praising the Lord after they won the battle against Sisera.

(cut 3)

Gideon

Banner Verses: "The angel of the LORD came and sat down under the oak . . . where []oash's] son Gideon was threshing wheat in a winepress to keep it from the Midianites. When the angel of the LORD appeared to Gideon, he said, 'The LORD is with you, mighty warrior'" (Judges 6:11–12).

As You Work: List here and talk about words, ideas, people, and questions the character and story bring to mind.

_____

_____

_____

_____

Supplies: patterns (square; oak leaf; acorn cap [cut 2 of same shade]; acorn nut [cut 2 of same shade]); felt (pumpkin; pirate green; cinnamon; walnut); dressmaker's scissors; pins; glue

Instructions: Match all pattern pieces to felt and cut out. Glue cap on each nut. Pin leaf and acorns in place; glue.

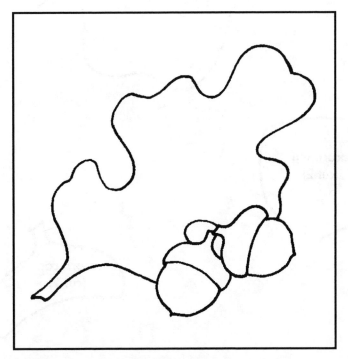

*As an acorn becomes a mighty oak, so Gideon
(the "least" in his family) became a mighty warrior.*

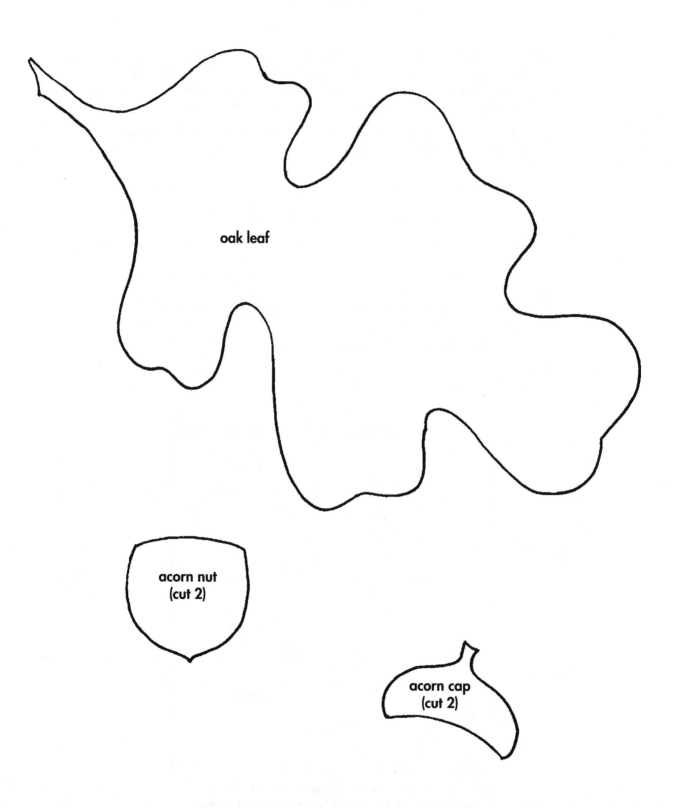

oak leaf

acorn nut
(cut 2)

acorn cap
(cut 2)

Jephthah

Banner Verses: "The Gileadites captured the fords of the Jordan leading to Ephraim, and whenever a survivor of Ephraim said, 'Let me cross over,' the men of Gilead asked him, 'Are you an Ephraimite?' If he replied, 'No,' they said, 'All right, say "Shibboleth."' If he said, 'Sibboleth,' because he could not pronounce the word correctly, they seized him" (Judges 12:5–6).

As You Work: List here and talk about words, ideas, people, and questions the character and story bring to mind.

_____

_____

_____

_____

Supplies: patterns (square; letters [10], arrow); felt (royal blue; 11 various-colored scraps); pins; glue; cuticle scissors; 3–3.5" circle (such as a lid)

Instructions: Match all pattern pieces to felt and cut out. Place circle in center of banner square; arrange and pin letters and arrow around it; remove circle. Glue letters and arrow, removing pins as you go.

*Clever Jephthah listened for colloquial pronunciation
to discover who were enemies.*

Ruth

Banner Verse: "So Boaz took Ruth and she became his wife. Then he went to her, and the LORD enabled her to conceive, and she gave birth to a son. . . . And they named him Obed. He was the father of Jesse, the father of David" (Ruth 4:13, 17b).

As You Work: List here and talk about words, ideas, people, and questions the character and story bring to mind.

_____

_____

_____

_____

Supplies: patterns (square; heart; braid strands [cut 3 shades]); felt (cinnamon; deep rose; butterscotch, soft beige, french vanilla); dressmaker's scissors; pins; glue

Instructions: Match square and heart pattern pieces to felt; cut out. Cut narrow braiding strands (3 shades) as long as possible—number needed will depend on tightness of braid. Starting at top V of heart, anchor (pin) 3 strands in each direction and braid. As you braid, shape and pin along heart edges, left and right. Interweave all pieces at bottom V; trim. Glue braid along heart edge; remove pins.

Headlines could have read "Gleaner Weds Grower" the day Ruth and Boaz exchanged vows.

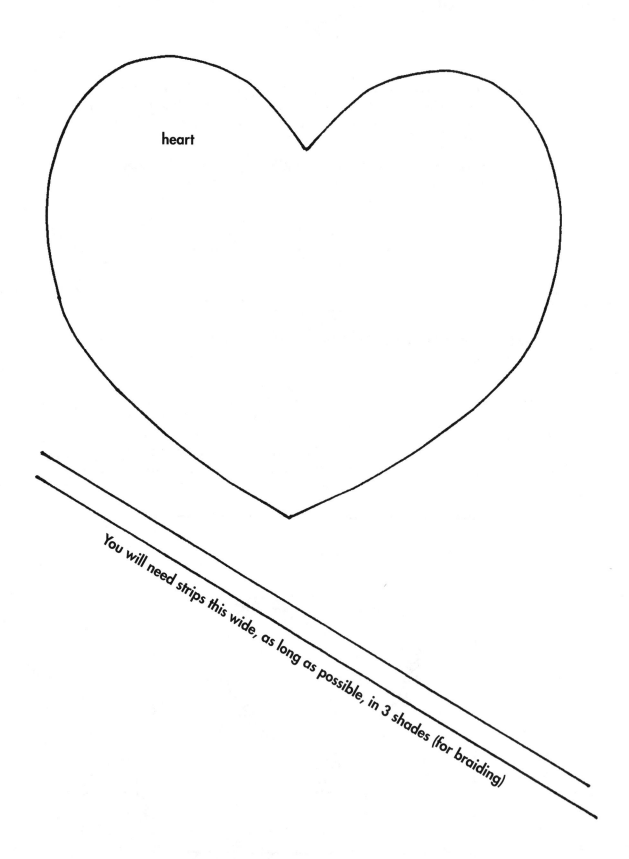

heart

You will need strips this wide, as long as possible, in 3 shades (for braiding)

Samson

Banner Verse: "Samson said, 'Let me die with the Philistines!' Then he pushed with all his might, and down came the temple on the rulers and all the people in it" (Judges 16:30).

As You Work: List here and talk about words, ideas, people, and questions the character and story bring to mind.

_____

_____

_____

_____

Supplies: patterns (square, shaft and base, fluting, base trim); felt (purple, soft beige, french vanilla, cashmere tan); dressmaker's scissors; pins; glue

Instructions: Match all pattern pieces to felt and cut out. Note dotted lines on fluting pattern; place pattern on felt and cut outside edges, then cut in 5 equal-width strips. Glue fluting strips equidistant on column. This is easiest if you glue the first two on the outer edges and the third in the middle (the remaining two are easy to place). Glue trim on base; glue base to shaft. "Break" column by making a zigzag cut through middle. Place column sections on square; glue. Trim excess at top edge. Cut "debris" from excess; glue near break.

Long known for physical might, Samson revealed strength of character the day he brought down the Philistines.

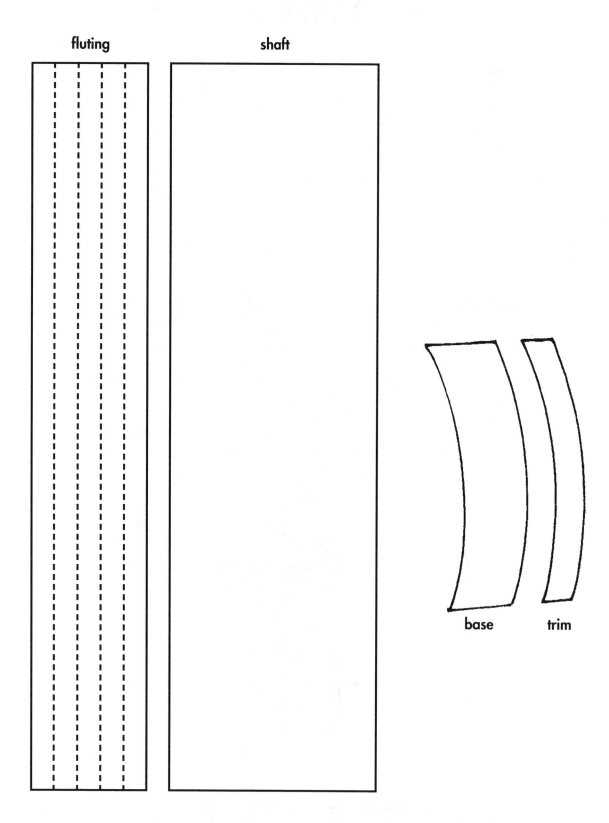

fluting

shaft

base   trim

Samuel

Banner Verse: "The lamp of God had not yet gone out, and Samuel was lying down in the temple of the LORD, where the ark of God was. Then the LORD called Samuel" (1 Samuel 3:3–4).

As You Work: List here and talk about words, ideas, people, and questions the character and story bring to mind.

_____

_____

_____

_____

Supplies: patterns (square, lamp, small flame, large flame); felt (sage, pumpkin, apricot, orange); dressmaker's scissors; pins; glue; cuticle scissors (optional)

Instructions: Match all pattern pieces to felt and cut out. (Hint: Cuticle scissors easily cut out lamp handle.) Assemble and glue flames. Pin parts on square; glue; remove pins.

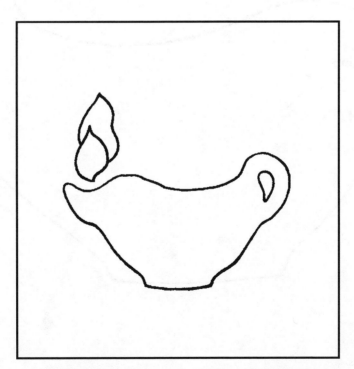

Samuel's early obedience to the Lord established a lifelong habit of listening to and following God.

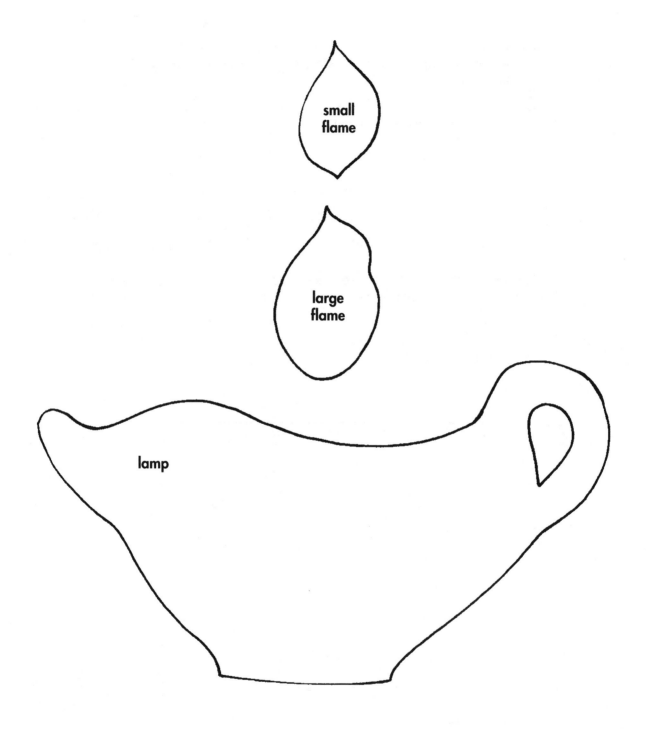

David

Banner Verse: "David was thirty years old when he became king, and he reigned forty years" (2 Samuel 5:4).

As You Work: List here and talk about words, ideas, people, and questions the character and story bring to mind.

_____

_____

_____

_____

Supplies: patterns (square; triangle [cut 2 shades]); felt (blueberry bash; gold, antique gold); dressmaker's scissors; pins; glue

Instructions: Match all pattern pieces to felt and cut out. Cut through dotted line on triangles. Interweave triangles as shown in illustration. Center and pin to square; glue, removing pins as you go. (Take care to close cut ends of triangles.)

Although David's life was often entangled, he emerged as a man after God's own heart.

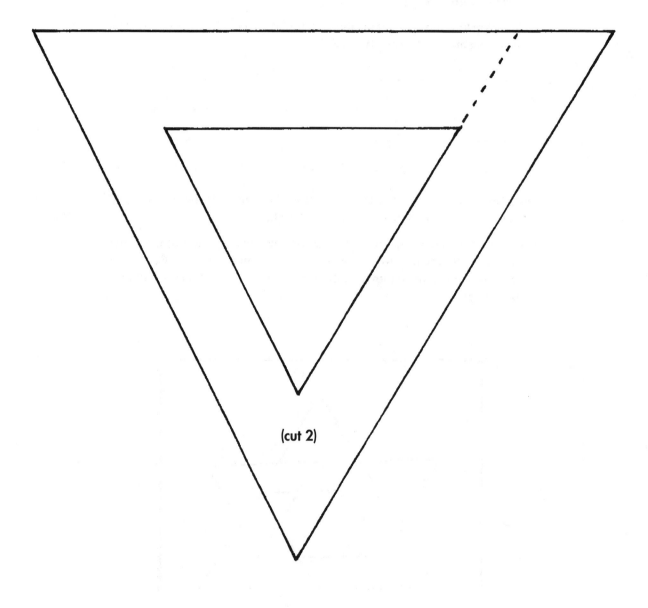

(cut 2)

Elijah

Banner Verse: "The ravens brought him bread and meat in the morning and bread and meat in the evening, and he drank from the brook" (1 Kings 17:6).

As You Work: List here and talk about words, ideas, people, and questions the character and story bring to mind.

_____

_____

_____

_____

Supplies: patterns (square, raven, brook, morsel); felt (grey, black, peacock, pumpkin); dressmaker's scissors; pins; glue

Instructions: Match all pattern pieces to felt and cut out. Glue brook to bottom of square, matching edges. Place raven with legs in brook; insert morsel in beak; glue all to square.

Elijah learned that sometimes the Lord takes care of his own in unusual ways.

ELIJAH—RAVEN PATTERN

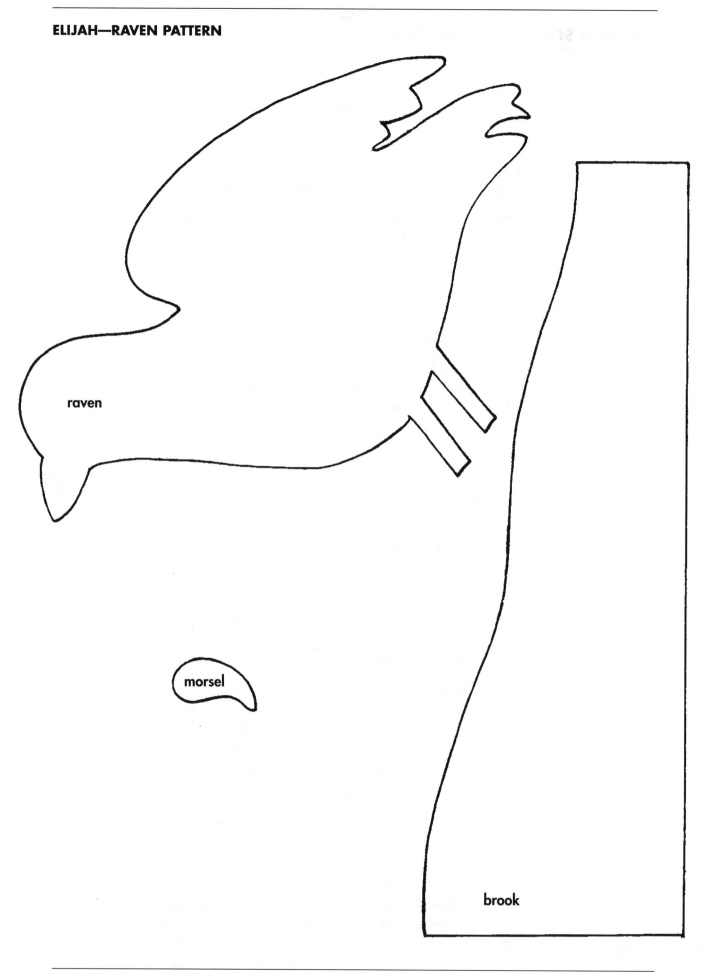

raven

morsel

brook

Elisha

Banner Verse: "Elisha said, 'Go around and ask all your neighbors for empty jars. Don't ask for just a few. . . . Pour oil into all the jars'" (2 Kings 4:3–4).

As You Work: List here and talk about words, ideas, people, and questions the character and story bring to mind.

_____

_____

_____

_____

Supplies: patterns (square; pots [4 shapes]); felt (apricot; sage, walnut, antique gold, harvest gold); dressmaker's scissors; pins; glue

Instructions: Match all pattern pieces to felt and cut out. Arrange pots and pin to square. Glue each pot to square (beginning with pot at the back of your arrangement), removing pins as you go.

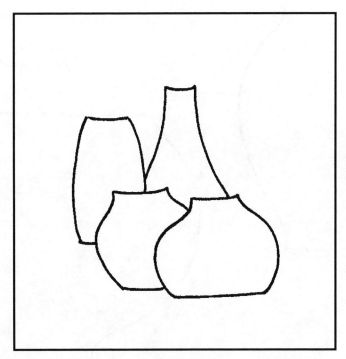

From the moment he asked for a double portion of the Lord's blessing, Elisha was known as a prophet with big ideas.

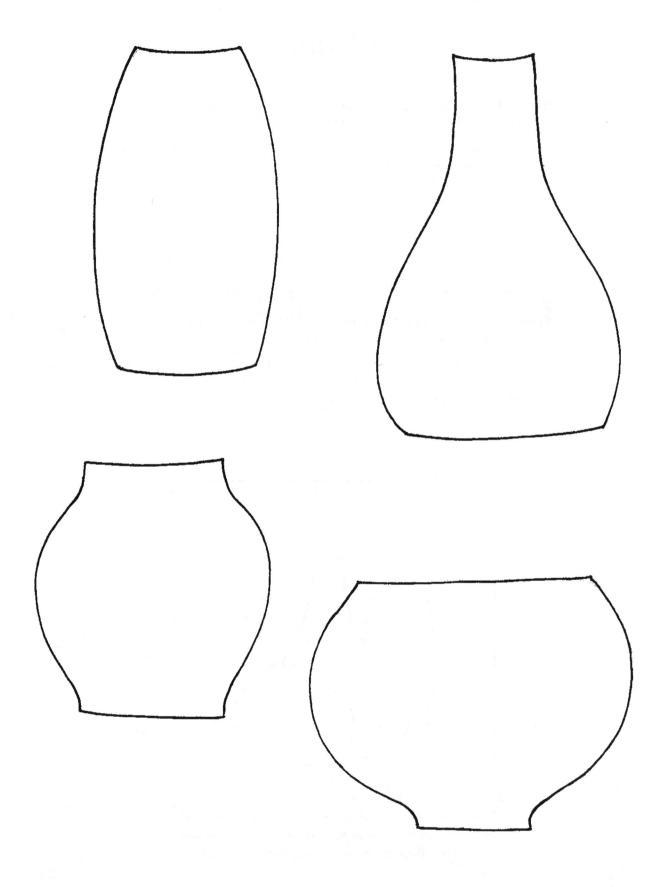

Jonah

Banner Verse: "But the LORD provided a great fish to swallow Jonah, and Jonah was inside the fish three days and three nights" (Jonah 1:17).

As You Work: List and talk about words, ideas, people, and questions the character and story bring to mind.

_____

_____

_____

_____

Supplies: patterns (square, fish, water, waterspout, figure); felt (charcoal, gray, cadet blue, white, color choice yours); dressmaker's scissors; pins; glue

Instructions: Match all pattern pieces to felt and cut out. Place water on square, matching side and bottom edges; glue. Glue figure to *back* of fish. Pin fish with blowhole out of water and figure hidden; glue. Insert waterspout; glue.

You cannot see him, but the creators of this banner square know Jonah is in the belly of the great fish.

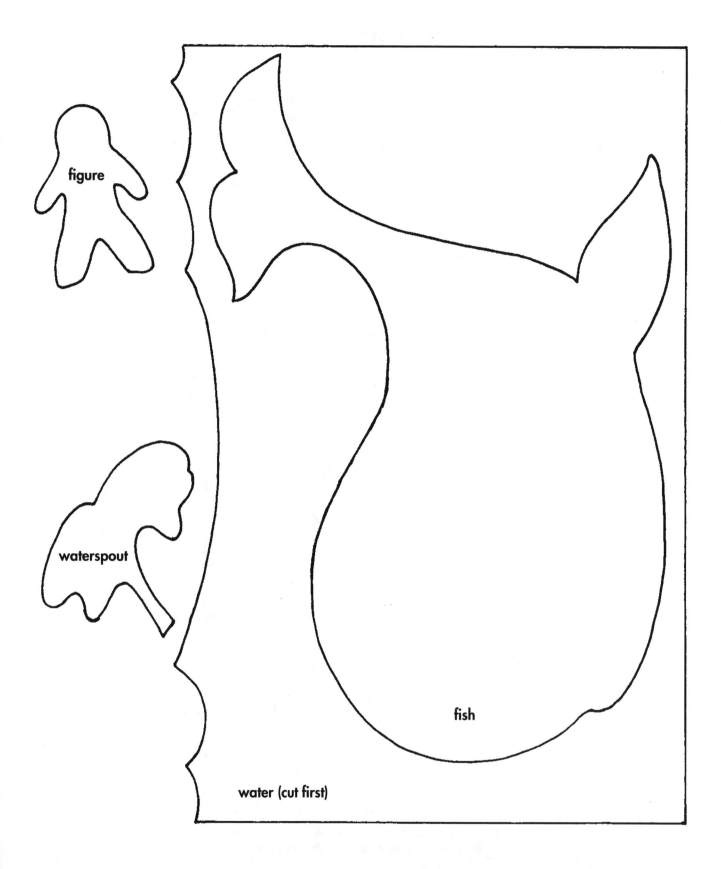

Isaiah

Banner Verse: "The desert and the parched land will be glad; the wilderness will rejoice and blossom" (Isaiah 35:1).

As You Work: List here and talk about words, ideas, people, and questions the character and story bring to mind.

_____

_____

_____

_____

Supplies: patterns (square; outer, middle, and center petals; leaf [cut 2 of same shade]); felt (baby pink; ruby, deep rose, ruby; leaf green); dressmaker's scissors; pins; glue; pinking shears (optional)

Instructions: Match all pattern pieces to felt and cut out. Cut leaf edges with pinking shears (optional). Layer and glue trio of flower parts to each other. Pin flower in center of square; tuck leaves underneath. Glue all to background, removing pins as you go.

Isaiah's many "growing" references include the blooming desert and the sprouting stump.

Daniel

Banner Verse: "My God sent his angel, and he shut the mouths of the lions. They have not hurt me" (Daniel 6:22).

As You Work: List here and talk about words, ideas, people, and questions the character and story bring to mind.

_____

_____

_____

_____

Supplies: patterns (square; lion [cut 3 shades]); felt (ruby; antique gold, cashmere tan, butterscotch); dressmaker's scissors; pins; glue

Instructions: Match all pattern pieces to felt and cut out. Layer and pin pieces to background (staggered as in illustration). Glue to background, removing pins as you go. Trim overhanging edges.

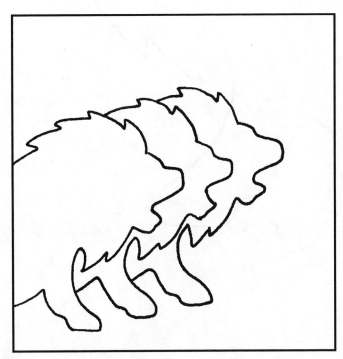

*The blood-red background hints at Daniel's fate
had God not shut the mouths of the lions.*

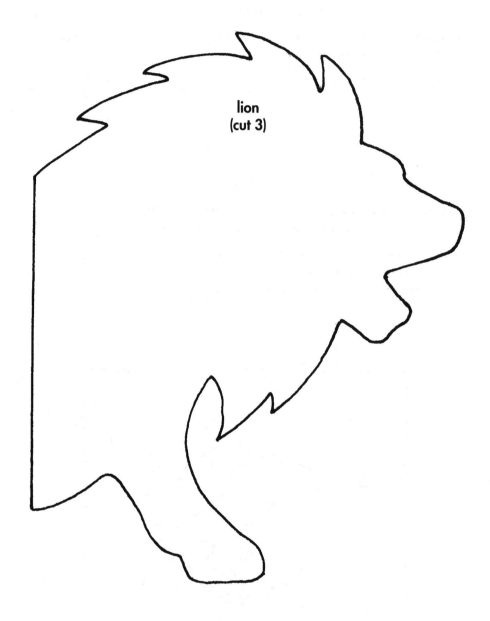

lion
(cut 3)

Esther

Banner Verse: "Now the king was attracted to Esther. . . . So he set a royal crown on her head and made her queen" (Esther 2:17).

As You Work: List here and talk about words, ideas, people, and questions the character and story bring to mind.

_____

_____

_____

_____

Supplies: patterns (square; sash [cut 2 of same shade], tiara; jewel [cut 3 shades]); felt (orchid; ruby; grey; blueberry bash, red, pirate green); dressmaker's scissors; pins; glue

Instructions: Match all pattern pieces to felt and cut out. Join sash halves and place diagonally from upper left to lower right corners of square; glue. Glue jewels to tiara points. Center tiara (covering sash seam) and glue to square.

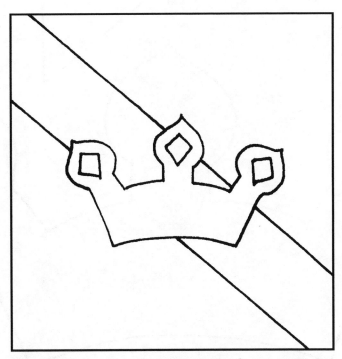

The sash and tiara acknowledged her beauty and position,
but courage and loyalty were Esther's true queenly attributes.

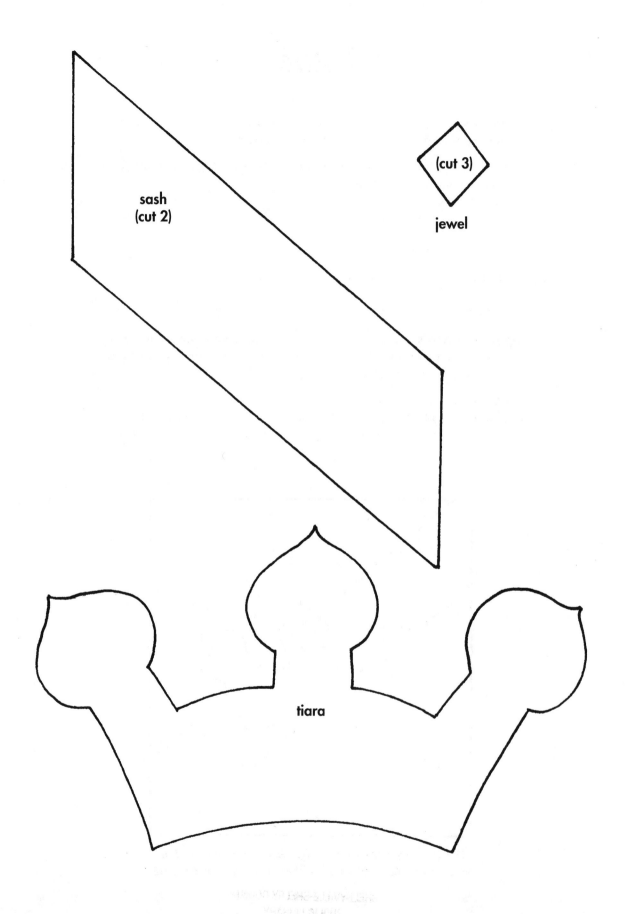

sash
(cut 2)

(cut 3)

jewel

tiara